DON'T BE DEVOURED

A FIELD GUIDE TO SPIRITUAL WARFARE:
EVERYDAY RHYTHMS • GOSPEL CONFIDENCE

DR. NIC WILLIAMS

DON'T BE DEVOURED

A Field Guide to Spiritual Warfare:
Everyday Rhythms • Gospel Confidence

IN HONOR OF MICHAEL JACOB

To **Michael**:
a man whose life preaches louder than words ever could.

A year ago, a stroke changed your world, but it didn't change your joy. It didn't dim your faith. It didn't quiet the light of Christ in you. Even now, as your voice waits to return, your life continues to speak, drawing people to Jesus and into our church family simply by the way you show up with courage, gratitude, and unwavering hope.

Your contagious joy, your steady presence, and your confidence in the goodness of God have inspired an entire church. This book is dedicated to you, Michael, with deep gratitude for the way your faith strengthens ours. May your story remind every reader that **the gospel shines brightest through a life anchored in Jesus.**

"BE ALERT AND OF SOBER MIND. YOUR ENEMY THE DEVIL PROWLS AROUND LIKE A ROARING LION LOOKING FOR SOMEONE TO DEVOUR."

1 PETER 5:8 (NIV)

CONTENTS

PART I
WAKE UP TO REALITY

THE LION IS REAL

In 2016, Lory and I moved into a home with a wideopen backyard that looked out over ponds and protected lands in Sarasota called the celery fields. It felt like a frontrow seat to creation. One still Florida evening, we sat on the back porch watching the sky melt from pink to purple, frogs singing, the air heavy, everything quiet, until it wasn't.

From somewhere beyond the tree line, a lion roared. We froze. Then another roar... and another, long, low, unmistakable. Even knowing there was a nearby refuge with big cats, your mind still runs through worst-case scenarios. Are the lions still caged? Did someone fall in? What is going on? In moments like that, something primal wakes up: your posture changes, your pulse jumps, your senses sharpen. In that moment, the quiet evening shifted. My body responded before my mind could because real danger wakes something in you.

Danger changes how you live. That is the spiritual point Peter won't let us ignore. He writes to ordinary believers with pastoral urgency: **"Be alert and of sober mind. Your enemy the devil prowls around like a roaring lion looking for someone to devour."** (1 Peter 5:8, NIV) The word "devour" isn't poetic flair; it names the enemy's aim: to consume faith, fracture families, and derail callings. But even here, Peter anchors vigilance in grace. In the same flow, he calls us to **"Humble yourselves, therefore, under God's mighty** hand, that he may lift you up in due time. Cast all your anxiety on him because he cares for you." (1 Peter 5:6-7, NIV) And he lifts our eyes with hope: "The God of all grace... will himself restore you and make you strong, firm and steadfast." (1 Peter 5:10, NIV) In other words, we keep our eyes open while we keep our burdens light, and we do both under a Father's care.

If you knew a lion had slipped loose in your neighborhood, your calendar would change. You wouldn't jog alone at dawn, leave the back door open, or send the kids out unsupervised. *Real threats demand real adjustments.* Spiritually, the same wisdom applies. We're not called to paranoia, but we are called to preparation, because paranoia paralyzes you, but preparation positions you to stand steady in a world with teeth.

When love gets casual (and why that's not love)

Danger doesn't just show up as an attack; sometimes it sneaks in through neglect. We're living in a moment where many parents, overcorrecting from a childhood of "forced religion," now outsource discipleship or let kids "decide for themselves." It feels gracious; it isn't. If you wouldn't let a child choose whether to buckle in during a crash, don't send them into spiritual traffic without guardrails. Scripture frames formation as daily, deliberate, relational: **"These commandments that I give you today are to be on your hearts. Impress them on your children... Talk about them when you sit at home and when you walk along the road, when you lie down and when you get up."** (Deuteronomy 6:6–7, NIV) That is not coercion; it's care. We don't force faith; we form hearts, on purpose, over time.

A real enemy, a better Savior

We err in two ditches, obsession (the devil is behind every inconvenience) and dismissal (nothing is spiritual; everything is "just human"). Jesus refuses both. He names a thief who comes **"only to steal and kill and destroy," and in the same breath announces His intent: **"I have come that they may have life, and have it to the full."** (John 10:10, NIV) We will name the enemy, but we will magnify Christ. That balance keeps us awake without becoming afraid.

Spiritual conflict is often hidden in the ordinary. Paul insists our struggle is not against people but **"against the spiritual forces of evil in the heavenly realms."** (Ephesians 6:12, NIV) Jesus treated that reality as concrete, not metaphor; He warned drowsy disciples, **"Watch and pray so that you will not fall into temptation. The spirit is willing, but the flesh is weak."** (Matthew 26:41, NIV) Awake, prayerful dependence is how courage keeps its eyes open.

And there's an order to this alertness that matters: **"Submit yourselves, then, to God. Resist the devil, and he will flee from you."** (James 4:7, NIV) Submission isn't passivity; it's alignment. We stand under God before we stand against evil, and that's why our resistance carries weight.

Reading the claw marks

Look around: chronic cynicism toward the church; confusion about identity; addictions that numb rather than heal; bitterness calcifying into isolation; spiritual apathy that seems polite but hollows the soul. These aren't random trends; they're claw marks, visible evidence of an invisible hunt. The enemy rarely shoves; he nudges. He doesn't always make people wicked; he's content to make them confused. So we learn to spot the "tall grasses" of modern life, isolation, hurry, small compromises, resentment, and noise, because that's where the ambush tends to hide.

Watchmen on the wall (prayer and planning together)

God has always called His people to alert love. In ancient cities, watchmen scanned the horizon and sounded the alarm. Nehemiah captured that balance beautifully: **"We prayed to our God and** posted a guard day and night to meet this threat." (Nehemiah 4:9, NIV) Later he notes that workers **"did their work with one hand and held a weapon in the other."** (Nehemiah 4:17, NIV) Prayer didn't replace preparation; it powered it. Gospel people aren't jittery; they're ready.

Peter's scarred wakeup call

Peter knew how quickly zeal can curdle into selfconfidence and how easily fear can drown out faith. He promised Jesus unwavering loyalty, collapsed under pressure, then met the risen Lord at a charcoal fire and was restored to shepherd. So when he writes, **"Be alert and of sober mind."** (1 Peter 5:8, NIV) he's not theorizing; he's pastoring from scars. That's good news for us: in Christ, your scars don't disqualify you; grace can redeploy them.

What this book will help you do

Across these pages, we'll wake up to the reality of the hunt, gear up with wisdom (not theatrics), fight together in community, and stand firm in hope because Jesus has already secured the decisive victory.

- You'll learn to recognize schemes without obsessing over them and to test invitations that look "good" but pull you from Christ (2 Corinthians 11:14, NIV).
- You'll build practical rhythms, Word, prayer, gathered worship, sane pace, honest community, that close the gaps where the lion crouches.
- You'll suit up in the armor where it belongs (Ephesians 6), not as religious imagery but as a daily, doable way of life.
- You'll help your family and church become watchful, joyful households that refuse both panic and passivity (Deuteronomy 6:6–7; Hebrews 10:24–25, NIV).
- Above all, you'll move with confidence because we don't fight for victory; we fight from it, under the banner of the cross where **Christ "disarmed the powers and authorities"**

(Colossians 2:15, NIV) and as citizens of a Kingdom where **"the Lion of the tribe of Judah... has triumphed."** (Revelation 5:5, NIV)

A practical beginning (start here this week)

- **Word before world.** Before news or notifications, read a short psalm aloud. Ask, "What is true about God here?"
- **Two-minute watch & pray.** Name one "tall grass" you'll face today (isolation? hurry? a familiar lie?). Pray, "Lord, keep me awake and dependent." (Matthew 26:41, NIV)
- **Submit → resist → replace.** When pressure hits, first align ("Jesus, Your authority"), then say no, then fill the space with something holy (a verse, a call to an ally, a brief gratitude walk). (James 4:7; Ephesians 6:17, NIV)
- **Don't walk alone.** Text one friend: "Can we check on each other twice this week?" Plan two five-minute calls.

REFLECTION & APPLICATION

- Where have you been living as if the lion isn't real? What "claw marks" tell you otherwise?

- Which "tall grass" hides your most common temptation, isolation, hurry, small compromises, resentment, or noise, and what single adjustment will you make this week?

- Who will stand watch with you in this season, and how will you invite them in?

The lion is real, but so is our hope. The enemy's roar may startle, yet the Lion of Judah has already triumphed. So lift your head, steady your heart, and walk alert, not afraid, **"for the one who is in you is greater than the one who is in the world."** (1 John 4:4, NIV)

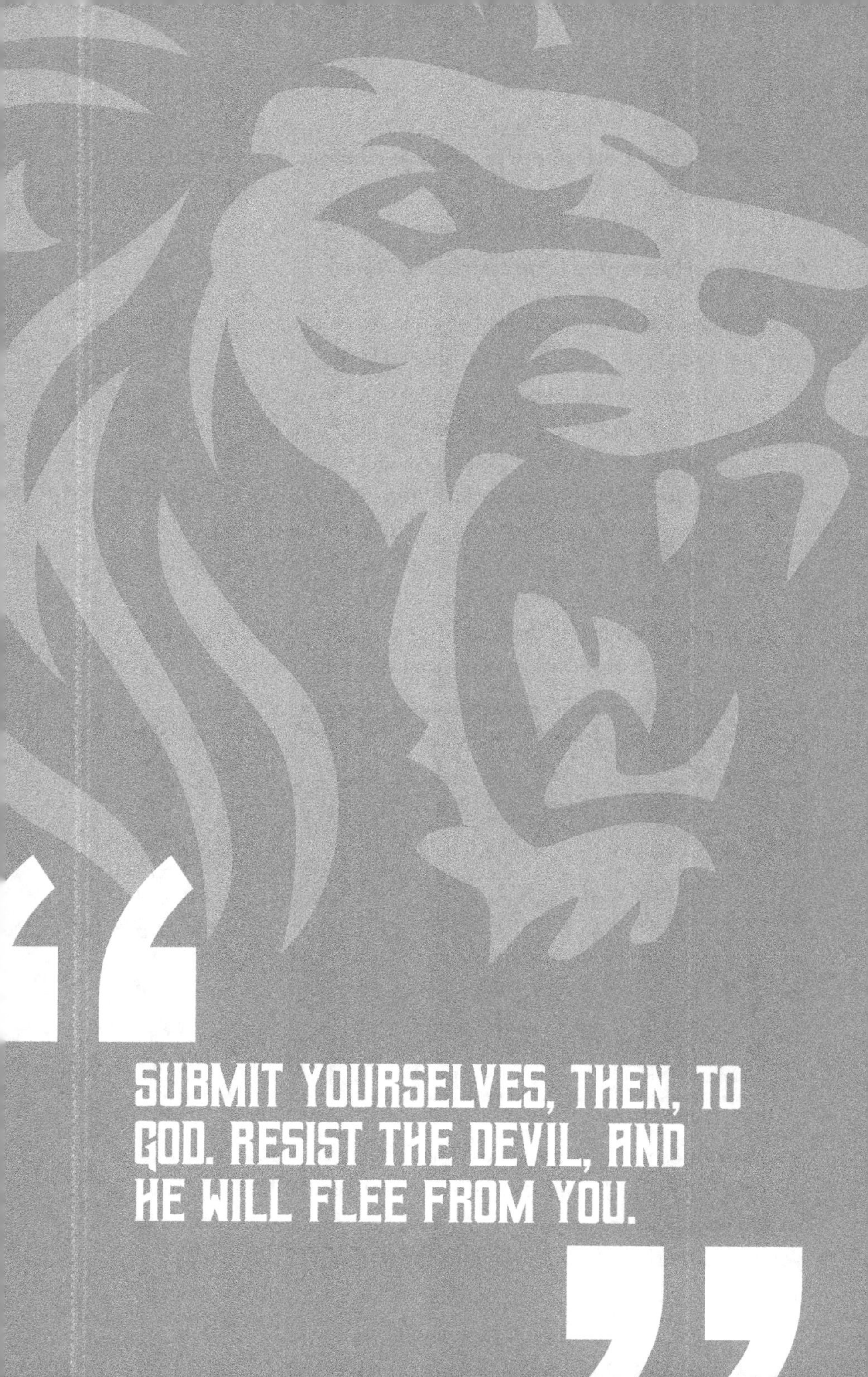
"
SUBMIT YOURSELVES, THEN, TO
GOD. RESIST THE DEVIL, AND
HE WILL FLEE FROM YOU.
"

CHAPTER 1

THE REALITY OF THE HUNT

Imagine again that lion roaming your neighborhood. You've seen the news alerts, the warning signs, maybe even heard the distant roar. Now, let's say your neighbor walks out his front door, earbuds in, completely unaware. He's strolling down the sidewalk like it's just another normal day. You call out to him, warning him of the danger, but he shrugs and says, "I don't see a lion." Moments later, he's blindsided.

Many Christians live their spiritual lives the same way, oblivious to the reality of the enemy. The Bible does not say the devil is like a distant threat, locked away and powerless. Instead, **1 Peter 5:8 (NIV)** warns us, **"Be alert and of sober mind. Your enemy the devil prowls around like a roaring lion looking for someone to devour."** The hunt is real. The danger is real. And yet, so many people walk through life as if they are entirely safe, unaware of the schemes of the enemy.

This is not just a casual warning. Peter is speaking from experience. This is the same man who promised Jesus he would never fall away, only to deny Him three times in a matter of hours. Peter knew firsthand what it meant to be blindsided by the enemy. When he tells us to be alert and sober-minded, it's not theological theory; it's personal testimony. It's a wake-up call from someone who's been knocked off his feet.

The devil isn't reckless, he's strategic. **Ephesians 6:11 (NIV)** urges us, **"Put on the full armor of God, so that you can take your stand against the devil's schemes."** Satan studies his prey. He observes your patterns, identifies your weaknesses, and targets the cracks in your spiritual armor. Like a lion, he waits silently, sometimes for years, for the moment when you're isolated, vulnerable, or spiritually sluggish.

Think about the story in **Genesis 3,** where Satan appears in the form of a serpent. He doesn't come with fire and fury, he comes with a question: *"Did God really say...?"* That subtle twist of truth was enough to sow doubt in Eve's heart. He didn't deny God's words outright; he simply distorted them. That's still how he operates today: quietly, deceptively, and with surgical precision.

Have you ever noticed that his attacks often come when you're tired: physically, emotionally, or spiritually? That's not a coincidence. He knows when your guard is down. In those moments, temptation feels stronger, lies sound more convincing, and resistance feels harder. He whispers subtle distortions like, "God doesn't really care about you," or "You've gone too far this time." **John 8:44 (NIV)** tells us, **"He is a liar and the father of lies."** His goal is always the same: to separate you from God by sowing seeds of doubt and discouragement.

Even more dangerous is how those lies often come cloaked in partial truths. **2 Corinthians 11:14 (NIV)** warns us, **"Satan himself masquerades as an angel of light."** That means sometimes deception comes looking like wisdom. It sounds logical. It even feels loving. That's the bait. He twists God's truth until it barely resembles what it was meant to be. C.S. Lewis captured this well when he wrote, *"The safest road to hell is the gradual one, the gentle slope, soft underfoot, without sudden turnings, without milestones, without signposts."*

Fast-forward to today, and nothing has changed. The enemy still uses the same playbook. One small compromise. One unanswered question. One moment of confusion. That's all it takes for the door to open.

Now, some argue that talking about the devil gives him too much credit. Others dismiss him altogether as a myth. But here's the truth: **denying the battle doesn't make it any less real. It only makes us unprepared. Hosea 4:6 (NIV)** says, **"My people are destroyed from lack of knowledge."** In other words, what we don't know can hurt us. Spiritual warfare is not just an occasional event; it is the context in which we live every day.

There's a reason **Ephesians 6:12 (NIV)** tells us, **"For our struggle is not against flesh and blood, but against the rulers, against the authorities, against the powers of this dark world and against the spiritual forces of evil in the heavenly realms."** That verse pulls back the curtain and reminds us there is a spiritual dimension to life that is very real.

So how do we stay alert? How do we keep from becoming easy prey?

First, we must recognize that this is a real battle with real stakes. **2 Corinthians 2:11 (NIV)** says, **"in order that Satan might not outwit us. For we are not unaware of his schemes."** Awareness is key. That's why spending time in God's Word and in prayer isn't optional; it's essential. It builds discernment. It gives you spiritual muscle memory so that when the lies come, you're ready. A daily walk with God isn't a checkbox. It's your defense plan.

Second, we need community. Lions hunt the stragglers. When you're alone, you're more vulnerable. But when you're surrounded by believers who love you, who pray for you, who hold you accountable, you're harder to take down. **Ecclesiastes 4:12 (NIV)** reminds us, **"Though one may be overpowered, two can defend themselves. A cord of three strands is not quickly broken."** Think about the value of trusted friends who will ask you the hard questions, call out your blind spots, and walk with you through spiritual battles.

Third, we must guard our vulnerabilities. Where are the soft spots in your life? Is it pride? Shame? Addiction? Fear? Satan aims for the weaknesses you try to hide. Don't pretend they're not there. Bring them into the light. Confess them. Strengthen those places with Scripture, support, and God's grace. A hidden weakness is like an open wound; it attracts the enemy.

Fourth, the enemy's attack is so subtle we don't even realize it's happening. He distracts us with busyness. He dulls our minds with entertainment. He desensitizes us with compromise. Before long, we're going through the motions, spiritually asleep, and wide open to attack. That's why Peter's call to be **"alert and of sober mind"** is so critical. Sobriety isn't just about abstaining from substances; it's about having a clear, focused mind, anchored in truth.

And finally, remember you are not alone in the fight. You don't overcome by grit. You are overcome by grace. I've sat with more than one believer who said, 'I never thought I'd end up here.' When we trace the story backward, it's rarely one big decision that takes them out. It's a slow drift, an ignored warning, a weakness left unguarded. That's why staying alert matters. **James 4:7 (NIV)** gives us this strategy: **"Submit yourselves, then, to God. Resist the devil, and he will flee from you."** It starts with surrender. God fights for you when you submit to Him. He equips you with His Spirit, His Word, and His people.

The truth is, Satan has power, but he does not have the final word. **Colossians 2:15 (NIV)** boldly declares, **"And having disarmed the powers and authorities, he made a public spectacle of them, triumphing over them by the cross."** Christ didn't just survive the hunt; He conquered it. And in Him, so do we.

The lion is real. But so is the victory. The first step is to stop pretending we're not in a fight. The second is to stand strong in the One who's already won.

So, are you alert? Are you aware? Or are you walking through life with spiritual earbuds in, hoping the danger stays far away? It's time to wake up. It's time to walk in truth, covered in grace, surrounded by others, and anchored in the victory of Jesus.

Because while the lion roars, the **Lion of Judah reigns**, and in Him, we are never alone in the hunt.

REFLECTION & APPLICATION

- Where have you seen signs of spiritual attack in your life recently? Looking back, were you alert to it or mostly unaware?

- What areas of your life feel the most vulnerable to the enemy's schemes, and what steps can you take to guard them?

- Who are the people in your life helping you stay spiritually strong, and how can you grow deeper in community and accountability with them?

The hunt is real, but so is our hope. The enemy may prowl, but he is not in control. Your job isn't to live scared, it's to live awake. Stay rooted in God's Word, surrounded by God's people, honest about your vulnerabilities, and confident in the One who has already won the victory. When you walk alert and anchored in Jesus, you're not easy prey, you're a protected son or daughter standing strong under the mighty hand of God.

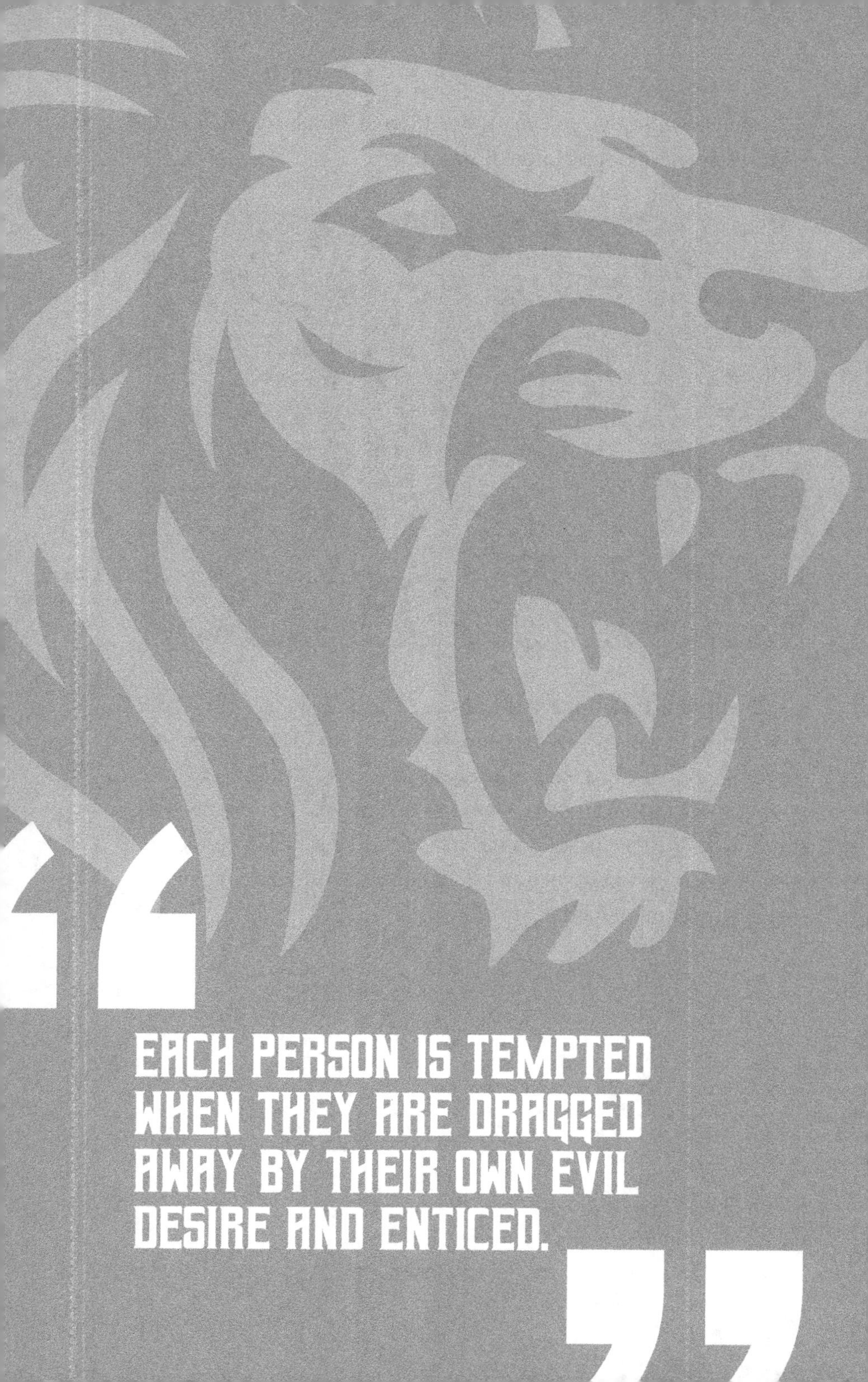
EACH PERSON IS TEMPTED WHEN THEY ARE DRAGGED AWAY BY THEIR OWN EVIL DESIRE AND ENTICED.

CHAPTER 2

THE DEVIL'S PLAYBOOK

Before any wise commander moves, he studies the adversary, tactics, patterns, and timing, so preparation beats panic when the moment arrives. One of the clearest pictures of this comes from General George S. Patton during World War II. Before the surprise German offensive known as the Battle of the Bulge, Patton had already anticipated the possibility of an attack. He wasn't just reacting, he was preparing. When the time came, he was ready. Through impossible winter conditions and logistical chaos, he rerouted his troops and turned the tide. Why? Because he studied the enemy and acted decisively.

I've heard it said before that ignorance isn't noble; it's reckless. **Strategy matters because schemes of the devil exist,** and the New Testament speaks so explicitly: **"Put on the full armor of God, so that you can take your stand against the devil's schemes."** (Ephesians 6:11, NIV) That single word, *schemes*, tells us the battle is planned, not random; personal, not generic; patient, not haphazard. Our goal in this chapter isn't to obsess over the enemy; it's to **recognize the pattern so we can reject the pull.**

Why "schemes" (not surprises) define the fight

From the Garden of Eden forward, the enemy repeats himself with ruthless consistency. He **deceives** to entice, **accuses** to immobilize, **divides** to isolate, and **distracts** to neutralize. Those are the big four.

Around them swirl a host of custom moves, comparison, self-pity, hurry, noise, each tailored to our particular vulnerabilities. **"Each person is tempted when they are dragged away by their own evil desire and enticed."** (James 1:14, NIV) In other words, the bait fits the appetite.

We'll walk through each tactic, then follow with counters grounded not in bravado but in Christ. We'll save the full "armor" deepdive for Chapter 6; for now, notice the order that steadies every response: **submit to God → resist the devil → replace the lie with truth** (cf. James 4:7; Ephesians 6:17, NIV). That sequence may be the most practical "play break" you ever call in the middle of a hard day.

Tactic 1: Deception (bending the truth till it breaks trust)

The first play in the book is as old as the garden. The serpent did not shove Eve; he **shifted** her: **"Did God really say...?"** (Genesis 3:1, NIV). The question looks harmless, even thoughtful, but it takes aim at God's character and Word. Jesus names the source: **"When he lies, he speaks his native language, for he is a liar and the father of lies."** (John 8:44, NIV) Paul adds the camouflage: **"Satan himself masquerades as an angel of light."** (2 Corinthians 11:14, NIV)

That last verse matters. The devil doesn't only push apparent evil; he **counterfeits the good**. He dresses self-indulgence as self-care, calls compromise compassion, and sprinkles halfverses into hollow advice. **The most dangerous lies are the ones that borrow holy words to bless unholy ends.**

How to counter: Slow down and test the invitation. *Where does this lead, toward Christ or away? Can I bring this into the light with a mature believer without euphemisms?* **"Everything exposed by the light becomes visible."** (Ephesians 5:13, NIV) If it needs the dark to survive, it isn't from the Lord.

Tactic 2: Temptation that feels custom-built

Temptation doesn't arrive as a generic offer; it shows up with a familiar tone and perfect timing. **"Each person is tempted when they are dragged away by their own evil desire and enticed."** (James 1:14, NIV) For one person, the hook is achievement; for another, it's affection, approval, control, escape, or ease. Notice the pattern you named: the hook is hidden in what appears to be relief or reward. **Sin often sells itself as a shortcut, around waiting, around obedience, around pain.**

Jesus shows the counter in the wilderness. Three times, He meets a twisted offer with unbending truth: **"It is written..."** (Matthew 4:1–11, NIV). He does not negotiate with hunger, bargain with power, or prove Himself on command. He **answers lies with Scripture** and **stays submitted to the Father**. That's our pattern: *submit → resist → replace*. **No temptation is unique, and God always provides a way out.** (see 1 Corinthians 10:13, NIV)

Tactic 3: Accusation (from seduction to shame)

He deceives on the front end, then prosecutes on the back end. Revelation calls him **"the accuser of our brothers and sisters"** (Revelation 12:10, NIV). The voice that said, *It's no big deal,* becomes the voice that says, *It's too big to forgive.* That swing is not an accident; **guilt weaponized into hopelessness** keeps you from running to the very grace that heals you.

Answer accusation with the gospel you believe for everyone else: **"Therefore, there is now no condemnation for those who are in Christ Jesus."** (Romans 8:1, NIV) Confession is not your fall from grace; it is how you fall into it: **"If we confess our sins, he is faithful and just and will forgive us our sins and purify us..."** (1 John 1:9, NIV) **When accusation shouts "unworthy," the cross answers "already covered."**

Tactic 4: Division (fracturing fellowship to weaken witness)

If he can't make you cave privately, he will try to make you collide publicly. **"If a house is divided against itself, that house cannot stand."** (Mark 3:25, NIV) Division rarely begins with doctrine; it begins with **unaddressed wounds, uncharitable assumptions, and unconfessed pride**. The New Testament's relentless "one another" commands exist because our unity is both fragile and powerful.

Paul's remedy is practical: **"Make every effort to keep the unity of the Spirit through the bond of peace."** (Ephesians 4:3, NIV) *Make every effort* means we choose slow words, fast forgiveness, and in-person conversations over digital escalation. **Unity isn't the absence of conflict; it's the presence of Christlike humility in conflict.**

Tactic 5: Distraction (good things crowding out the Best)

Sometimes the scheme is not scandal but **static**. Fill your mind with notifications, your calendar with noise, your heart with hurry, and the enemy doesn't need to defeat you; he can just **dilute** you. Jesus' words to Martha still read like a diagnosis for our age: **"You are worried and upset about many things, but few things are needed, or indeed only one."** (Luke 10:41-42, NIV)

Paul's counsel gives us a counterrhythm: **"Be very careful, then, how you live, not as unwise but as wise, making the most of every opportunity..."** (Ephesians 5:15-16, NIV) That's not legalism; that's love stewarding attention. **What wins your attention will shape your affection.**

Tactic 6: Discouragement and despair (fog over the field)

After big faith moments, discouragement can feel like whiplash. Elijah called down fire, then ran into the wilderness, sure he was alone and finished. God's answer did not scold his exhaustion; it met it, rest, food, presence, perspective, and people (1 Kings 19). **Despair shrinks reality to the size of your feelings; God's presence**

widens it to the size of His faithfulness. When the fog thickens, pray the psalmist's stubborn refrain: **"Why, my soul, are you downcast? ... Put your hope in God."** (Psalm 42:5, NIV)

Tactic 7: Counterfeit "good" (angeloflight offers)

The enemy often sidles up posing as help, a soothing narrative that baptizes compromise with kind words. **"Satan himself masquerades as an angel of light"** (2 Corinthians 11:14, NIV). Learn to ask: Is this compassion that empties truth, or compassion that tells the truth in love? Real grace doesn't lie to make you feel better; it tells the truth to set you free (John 8:32, NIV).

Recognizing the Voices (a quick discerner)

The Shepherd's voice always **draws**, never drives. He speaks with love and conviction, leading you toward Jesus, while the enemy presses with guilt and shame to push you away. The Shepherd brings clarity shaped by Scripture, the enemy stirs confusion and slippery rationalizations. The Shepherd offers grace and a next step; the enemy whispers doom and insists you're trapped. The Shepherd calls you into community and light, the enemy urges secrecy and isolation. The Shepherd builds and blesses; the enemy tears down, taunts, and devours.

Learning the difference doesn't require mystical sensitivity; it requires Scripture, honesty, and community. Test every voice by the truth of God's Word, then bring it into the light with trusted believers. Discernment is not guesswork; it's attention shaped by truth and confirmed in fellowship.

VOICE DISCERNER: "Draws vs. Drives" (Quick Check)

If you're ever unsure whether a thought is from God or from the enemy, this quick discerner can help. God's voice draws; the enemy's voice drives, and the differences are clearer than you think.

- **Draws** with love & *specific* conviction → **Drives** with guilt, shame, or vague condemnation
- **Draws** you *toward* Jesus & His people → **Drives** you *away* into isolation
- **Draws** with clarity and truth → **Drives** with confusion and distortion
- **Draws** by offering grace & hope → **Drives** by declaring you're stuck and hopeless
- **Draws** to obedient next steps → **Drives** with panicked urgency or perfectionism

I've included an exercise in the Appendix of this book to help you determine the voice you are listening to.

Counters that actually work (Jesus-shaped responses)

Awareness matters, but action is what keeps you standing. When the pressure hits, these Jesus-centered responses give you something solid to reach for, moves that quiet the lies, steady your heart, and pull you back into the light.

1) Submit, then resist, then replace. The order matters: **"Submit yourselves, then, to God. Resist the devil, and he will flee from you."** (James 4:7, NIV) Start by aligning under Christ's authority in prayer. Then resist the specific lie or lure. Then **replace** the empty space with something holy, read a psalm aloud, call an ally, serve someone, or take a gratitude walk. *If you don't replace, old patterns return.*

2) Answer lies with Scripture. Don't out-argue a tempter; out-truth him. Keep three verses ready, one for fear (e.g., **"The Lord is my light and my salvation, whom shall I fear?"** Psalm 27:1, NIV), one for identity (**"See what great love the Father has lavished on us..."** 1 John 3:1, NIV), one for temptation (**"[He] will also provide a way out..."** 1 Corinthians 10:13, NIV). Speak them **out loud** when the pressure spikes.

3) Practice pre-decisions. I have been sharing this one since I was a youth pastor, and there is so much power in this concept.

Decide **before** the moment what you'll do **in** the moment: where your phone sleeps, who you text when you're triggered, which rooms you won't enter online, and how you'll bow out of unwise settings. **Pre-decisions turn "I'll try" into "I already chose."**

4) Close the isolation gap. The schemes thrive in secrecy, so shrink it. Who gets your "ground is tilting" text? Who has permission to ask anything, anytime? **"Confess your sins to each other and pray for each other so that you may be healed."** (James 5:16, NIV)

5) Watch and pray (not panic and post). Jesus' rhythm still works: **"Watch and pray so that you will not fall into temptation."** (Matthew 26:41, NIV) Watch with your eyes (notice the setup). Pray with your dependence (invite the Spirit's help). **Panic is not a fruit of the Spirit; power, love, and self-discipline are.** (see 2 Timothy 1:7, NIV)

6) Keep a short account with God. When you stumble, run **toward** Him, not away. **"There is now no condemnation for those who are in Christ Jesus."** (Romans 8:1, NIV) Confess, receive cleansing, and take the way out next time. **Grace is not lenience; it is the power to stand back up.**

Case windows (how the plays show up on Tuesdays)

Schemes don't just live in the abstract; they show up in real lives, in ordinary moments, on the kinds of Tuesdays that feel predictable until they aren't. Most people don't wake up planning to compromise, isolate, or drift. The enemy works slowly, subtly, and strategically, nudging rather than shoving. These brief case windows show how the devil's playbook plays out in everyday life and how grace breaks the cycle when light gets in.

The negotiated boundary. It always starts small. "We'll just text late, not meet." It feels innocent, an exception, not a pattern. But minor exceptions become new norms, and soon the boundary has shifted, and so has integrity. Eventually, the person admitted that the "exception" had been the plan all along. The turning point came when they brought it into the light, redrew the line in community, and refused secrecy its oxygen. **Light breaks lies; secrecy feeds them.**

The success spiral. A leader strings together a season of wins and feels unstoppable. God doesn't get rejected; He just gets rescheduled. Quietly, the whisper comes: "You deserve this." The fatigue feels like freedom. But beneath the momentum is a soul running on fumes. The breakthrough didn't come from more success; it came when the leader restored Sabbath, invited honest feedback, and remembered that achievement is a poor anesthetic for an empty heart.

The offended heart. One small comment, careless, not cruel, lodges deeper than expected. Instead of being addressed, it's replayed. A story begins to form: "They meant to hurt me. They always do." Days become weeks, and what started as a moment hardens into a narrative that calcifies the relationship. The turnaround came through Matthew 18 obedience: a face-to-face conversation, slow words, quick forgiveness, and the Spirit's peace settling where resentment once lived.

A note on power and limits

Don't inflate the adversary. He is not God's equal. He is created, bounded, and ultimately judged. **"The one who is in you is greater than the one who is in the world."** (1 John 4:4, NIV) That doesn't minimize the roar; it **maximizes the reign** of Christ. And because Jesus already **"disarmed the powers and authorities... triumphing over them by the cross"** (Colossians 2:15, NIV), you are not trying to scrape together a win; **you are applying a victory.**

Field Drill (this week's practice)

Name your top two baits. Where does temptation most often hook you (approval, comfort, control, escape, envy)? Write them down. Pair each with a verse you will speak when the pull begins.

Write your pre-decisions. One boundary for screens, one for schedule, one for solitude with God. Share them with your ally.

Build your "way of escape" script. Pre-type a text you'll send when pressure spikes: "Ground is tilting, please call me now." Keep it pinned. (see 1 Corinthians 10:13, NIV)

Morning alignment, evening review. AM: submit (James 4:7), ask for alert eyes, read one psalm. PM: Where did the enemy try deception, accusation, division, or distraction? How did you respond? Thank God for grace; plan tomorrow's adjustments.

REFLECTION & APPLICATION

- Which of the four big schemes, **deceive, accuse, divide, distract**, hits you most predictably right now, and what would "submit → resist → replace" look like in that moment?

- Which *voice test* line helped you the most this week (draws vs. drives, clarity vs. confusion, grace vs. doom)? Where will you practice it tomorrow?

- What pre-decision (boundary or rhythm) would close a door you keep leaving cracked for temptation?

You don't need to memorize a thousand plays; **you need to master the counters**, submit to God, answer with Scripture, and move in the light with God's people. The schemes aren't new, **but your Savior is near**, and His Word still sends the tempter fleeing.

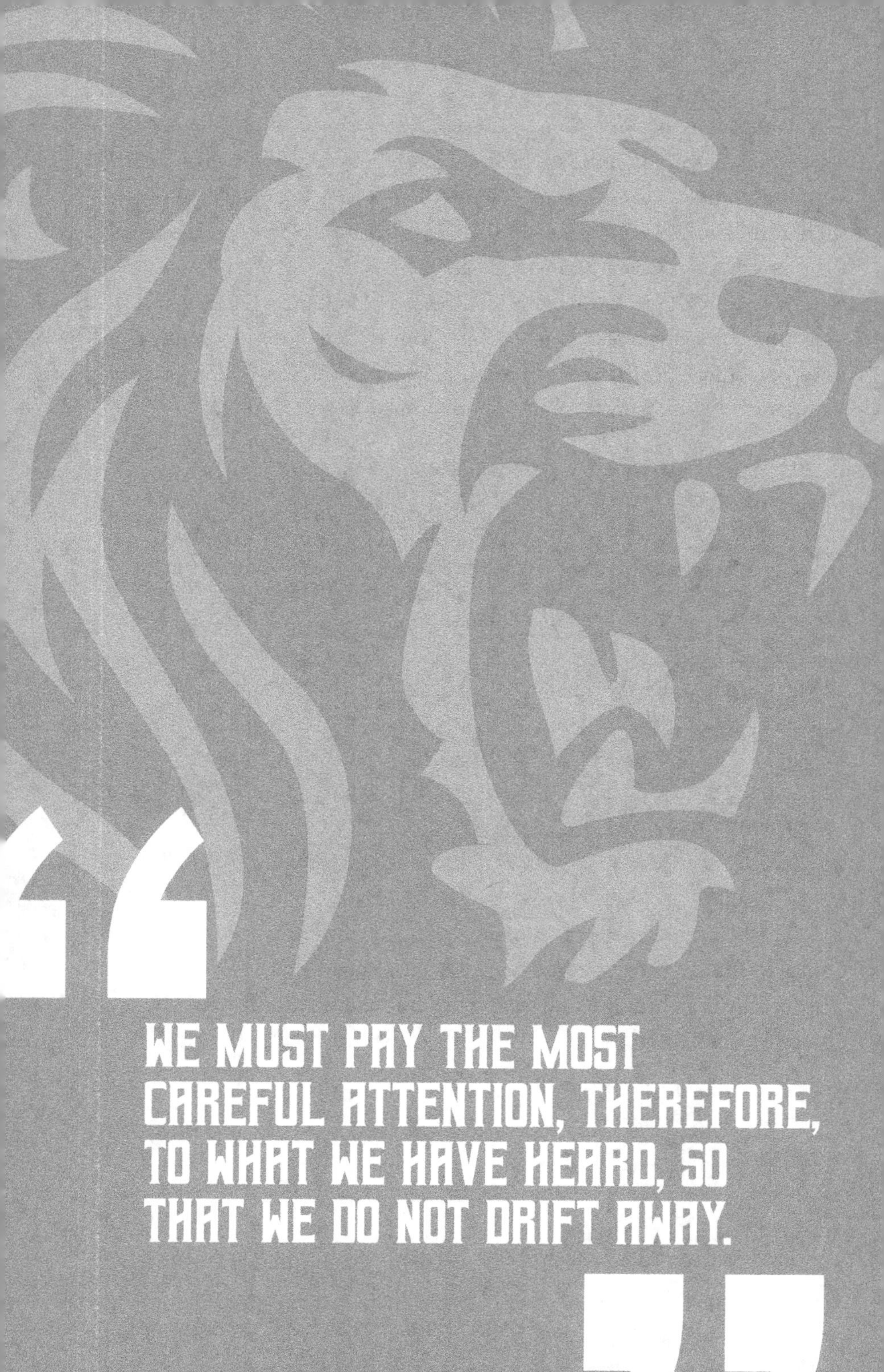
"
WE MUST PAY THE MOST CAREFUL ATTENTION, THEREFORE, TO WHAT WE HAVE HEARD, SO THAT WE DO NOT DRIFT AWAY.
"

CHAPTER 3

THE COST OF IGNORING THE THREAT

You can ignore a storm warning, but the storm won't ignore you. During our first Florida hurricane season, I watched neighbors split into two camps: some boarded windows, filled sandbags, and checked on the elderly down the street; others shrugged and left the patio furniture out. That first long, windy night taught me something: **minimizing a real threat doesn't make you safer...it makes you unprepared.** Those nights "riding out the wind and rain" became a classroom in vigilance, an almost one-to-one picture of the spiritual life.

This chapter is about that exact moment between the alert and your response. Peter has already told us to live awake, not anxious; the point here is practical and pastoral: **when we ignore the spiritual threat, drift follows, vulnerability increases, and joy erodes.** Not because God withholds grace, but because we stop receiving it.

How drift really happens

Drift is rarely dramatic. It's incremental, almost polite. We skip a few mornings in the Word, put prayer on "when I get to it," slide out of our group for a few weeks, and assume nothing changed. Scripture says otherwise: **"We must pay the most careful attention, therefore, to what we have heard, so that we do not drift away."** (Hebrews 2:1, NIV) Notice the language, *pay the most careful attention.* In other words, the default setting of a soul in a fallen world isn't spiritual momentum; it's spiritual drift.

The Bible pictures drift like a slow encroachment. The writer of Proverbs shows a field overrun not overnight but by neglect: thorns creeping, walls crumbling, poverty arriving "like a bandit." The warning fits our inner life: **neglect is not neutral; it's formative.** Left unattended, desires deform, habits harden, and hope thins.

The trouble is that drift often feels like rest. We call withdrawal "margin," numbness "peace," and indifference "maturity." **When apathy starts wearing spiritual clothing, alarms should sound.**

What ignoring the threat costs

Ignoring the spiritual threat carries real costs, and the first is increased vulnerability to familiar temptations. Temptation hunts for low guardrails and tired hearts, and Jesus named the pattern plainly: **"Watch and pray so that you will not fall into temptation. The spirit is willing, but the flesh is weak."** (Matthew 26:41, NIV) When watchfulness fades and prayer thins, the same old lures begin to feel inevitable. It's not that the fight gets harder; it's that we grow quieter.

A second cost is a shrinking, heavier life. Jesus calls us into fullness, not mere survival, but when we live inattentive to our souls, life turns all weight and no music. Desire loses its direction, calling drifts to the margins, and obedience begins to feel optional. This is the slow fade from joy into "just getting by." Ignoring the threat rarely explodes into scandal; more often, it settles into smallness.

We also pay the price in our relationships. Unchecked irritations calcify into resentments. Gaps go unclosed. We grow quick to interpret motives and slow to confess our own faults. Scripture warns that a "root of bitterness" can grow up and "defile many." (Hebrews 12:15, NIV) Living unalert doesn't just make us vulnerable; it makes us less safe for the people around us.

And finally, ignoring the threat dulls the conscience. Paul describes those who, "having lost all sensitivity," slip into whatever feels good in the moment. (Ephesians 4:19, NIV) That kind of numbness doesn't start with rebellion; it begins with rationalization. Repeated neglect slowly numbs what the Spirit is trying to keep tender. Drift rarely looks dramatic at first, but its costs run deep.

Why we look away (and what to do instead)

If vigilance matters so much, why do so many of us struggle to stay awake? Often, it's because the things that pull our attention feel familiar, comforting, or even wise in the moment. Naming these patterns helps us replace them with something better.

Hurry feels holy. Busyness impersonates importance. It's easy to confuse a jammed calendar with a faithful life, until we hear Jesus' gentle correction to Martha: **"You are worried and upset about many things, but few things are needed, or indeed only one."** (Luke 10:41–42, NIV) Choose the "one" first; then do the many.

Cynicism feels safe. After disappointments, "awake" can start to sound like naïveté. But cynicism is just fear wearing a mask of intelligence. Paul's counsel cuts through it: **"Be very careful, then, how you live, not as unwise but as wise."** (Ephesians 5:15, NIV) Wisdom isn't naive; it's alert love in motion.

Overconfidence feels spiritual. **"So, if you think you are standing firm, be careful that you don't fall!"** (1 Corinthians 10:12, NIV) Overconfidence mistakes yesterday's encounter with God for today's endurance in God. **Spiritual strength is replenished, not presumed.**

Shame feels like humility. After a stumble, many believers hide. But shame selfprotects; humility seeks help. **"There is now no condemnation for those who are in Christ Jesus."** (Romans 8:1, NIV) **The gospel does not minimize sin; it maximizes grace where we bring sin into the light.**

Wake-up calls in Scripture

If drift is subtle, God's wake-up calls are mercifully loud. To a dozing church, Jesus says, **"Wake up! Strengthen what remains** and is about to die." (Revelation 3:2, NIV) Paul writes, **"The hour has already come for you to wake up from your slumber."** (Romans 13:11, NIV) These are not scoldings but summons, **alerts from love**.

Peter's own life adds weight to the call. The man who fell asleep in Gethsemane later wrote about sober-minded alertness, not to scare us, but to shepherd us back to sanity. He knew how fast zeal can sour into self-confidence and how faithfully Jesus restores the repentant.

Sarasota stormprep, soulprep (a field checklist)

I live where people know how to prepare: board the windows, clear the yard, fuel the generator, and agree on check-ins. That muscle memory preaches. Here's a spiritual stormprep built from that wisdom:

- **Secure the windows (guard your inputs).** Before you face the day's wind, decide what gets access to your attention. Paul's grid still holds: **"Whatever is true... noble... right... pure... think about such things."** (Philippians 4:8, NIV) Curate on purpose.
- **Stack the sandbags (strengthen weak spots).** Name the low doorway, the latenight scrolling, the afterconflict selfpity, the travelweek loneliness. Then stack boundaries there. **"Clothe yourselves with the Lord Jesus Christ, and do not think about how to gratify the desires of the flesh."** (Romans 13:14, NIV)
- **Check the flashlight (keep Scripture at hand). "Your word is a lamp for my feet, a light on my path."** (Psalm 119:105, NIV) Keep three verses ready: fear, identity, temptation. Speak them **out loud** when pressure spikes.
- **Fuel the generator (sustain prayer and worship).** When the power flickers, you don't scramble for a manual; you start the backup you primed yesterday. **"Devote yourselves to prayer, being watchful and thankful."** (Colossians 4:2, NIV)

Gratitude is often the starter rope.

- **Confirm the contact list (reduce isolation).** Set who gets the "ground is tilting" text. **"Let us consider how we may spur one another on... not giving up meeting together... but encouraging one another."** (Hebrews 10:24-25, NIV)
- **Know the evacuation route (flee what you can't fight).** Sometimes victory is a U-turn. **"Flee the evil desires of youth and pursue righteousness..."** (2 Timothy 2:22, NIV) **You're not weak for leaving; you're wise.**

Preparation isn't panic; it's love in advance. Build these before the winds rise, not during.

Case windows: what ignoring looks like on Tuesdays

Here are a few snapshots of what ignoring the threat looks like in real life, ordinary people on ordinary days drifting further than they meant to.

The quiet quit. A faithful volunteer begins "taking a break" from serving, which is reasonable at first, but then drifts from the community altogether. The symptoms: muted appetite for Scripture, brittle responses to minor offenses, unexplained fatigue. Turning point: a candid coffee with a smallgroup leader, a simple rule of life (Word before world, one weekly table with believers), and two honest check-ins. Within weeks, oxygen returns.

The steady, successful parent. Work thrives, family calendar is full, church attendance is decent, yet the soul is loud with hurry and thin on prayer. The "threat" doesn't look like a scandal; it looks like spiritual malnutrition. Turning point: reanchoring mornings (Psalm in the chair, phone in the kitchen), Sabbath without apology, and **one** nightly question at the table: "Where did you see God at work today?"

The strong young leader. Gifted communicator, sincere heart, always "on." Quietly, envy and comparison gnaw at joy. The drift shows up as compulsive checking, prickly insecurity, and defensiveness. Turning point: confessing envy to a mentor (James 5:16), deleting metrics for a month, memorizing **"A man can receive only what is given him from heaven."** (John 3:27, NIV) Peace starts to outrun pressure.

In each story, there was no spectacular ambush, **just unattended doors.** Closing them wasn't complicated; it was consistent.

A path back when you've been drifting

Drift doesn't need drama to reverse; it needs direction. Here's the path home.

1. Remember, then repent, then redo. Jesus' counsel to Ephesus is gentle and surgical: **"Consider how far you have fallen! Repent and do the things you did at first."** (Revelation 2:5, NIV) Remember the early practices that woke your heart, then actually do them again. **Nostalgia won't heal you; obedience will.**

2. Trade vagueness for truth. Name the compromise out loud to God and a trusted believer. **"If we confess our sins, he is faithful and just and will forgive us our sins and purify us."** (1 John 1:9, NIV) Clarity breaks the spell.

3. Rebuild with small, durable rhythms. Big plans impress; small plans endure. Ten unhurried minutes in the Word daily will outlast occasional heroic hours. **Faithfulness is slow strength.**

4. Invite pressuretested people close. Ask two believers to ask you anything for a month. **"Carry each other's burdens, and in this way you will fulfill the law of Christ."** (Galatians 6:2, NIV) You are not a burden; you are the Body.

5. Hold your horizon. Israel forgot who fought for them when they stared at giants. We do, too. Isaiah's word steadies our pace: **"In repentance and rest is your salvation, in quietness and trust is your strength."** (Isaiah 30:15, NIV) **Strength returns where striving yields to trust.**

From hurricane alleys to spiritual battlefields, the lesson repeats: **what you ignore will eventually injure you.** You don't need to live clenched or suspicious; you do need to live awake. Grace is not fragile; it's simply meant to be received daily, not presumed weekly. In Peter's language, soberminded doesn't mean somberhearted. It means eyes open, hands open, life open to the God who keeps His people.

And yes, you will still have nights when the wind howls and the house creaks. The point isn't avoiding weather; it's abiding in the One who calms it. The goal isn't a threatfree life; **it's a prepared, joyful, nonnaive life**, a life that takes both the enemy and the gospel seriously, in that order.

Field Drill (this week)

- **Do a "drift audit."** Circle three domains, Word, Prayer, Community, and rate attention (1–5). Name one concrete adjustment for the lowest number (e.g., Psalm aloud before phone; 10minute evening prayer walk; text your group leader to reengage).
- **Write your stormprep card.** On one index card (or phone note), list: your three Scriptures (fear/identity/temptation), your two allies with numbers, your one boundary you'll honor this week. Read it morning and evening.
- **Practice a daily "submit → resist → replace."** In the next pressure moment: **submit** to Christ's authority (in words), **resist** the specific lie, **replace** it with an embodied act (read a verse aloud, step outside and thank God for five gifts, call your ally).
- **Sabbath a screen.** Choose one 24hour window this week with news and social off. Fill the space with presence, Scripture, people, rest.

REFLECTION & APPLICATION

- Where have you quietly renamed drift as "rest" or "margin"? What does honest naming change this week?

- Which cost are you feeling most, vulnerability, smallness, strained relationships, or a dulled conscience, and what first step will address it?

- Who needs to be on your contact list when the "ground is tilting," and how will you invite them into that role today?

- Which item on the stormprep checklist is most urgent for your household right now, windows, sandbags, flashlight, generator, contact list, or evacuation route?

You don't need to roar louder than the lion; you need to **live more awake than the world**, eyes up, hands open, heart anchored. You can't keep storms from forming, but you can stop pretending skies are clear when they're not. The cost of ignoring the threat is always higher than the cost of getting ready. So prepare in love, walk in light, and expect the Shepherd to steady you when the winds rise.

PART II
GEAR UP WITH WISDOM

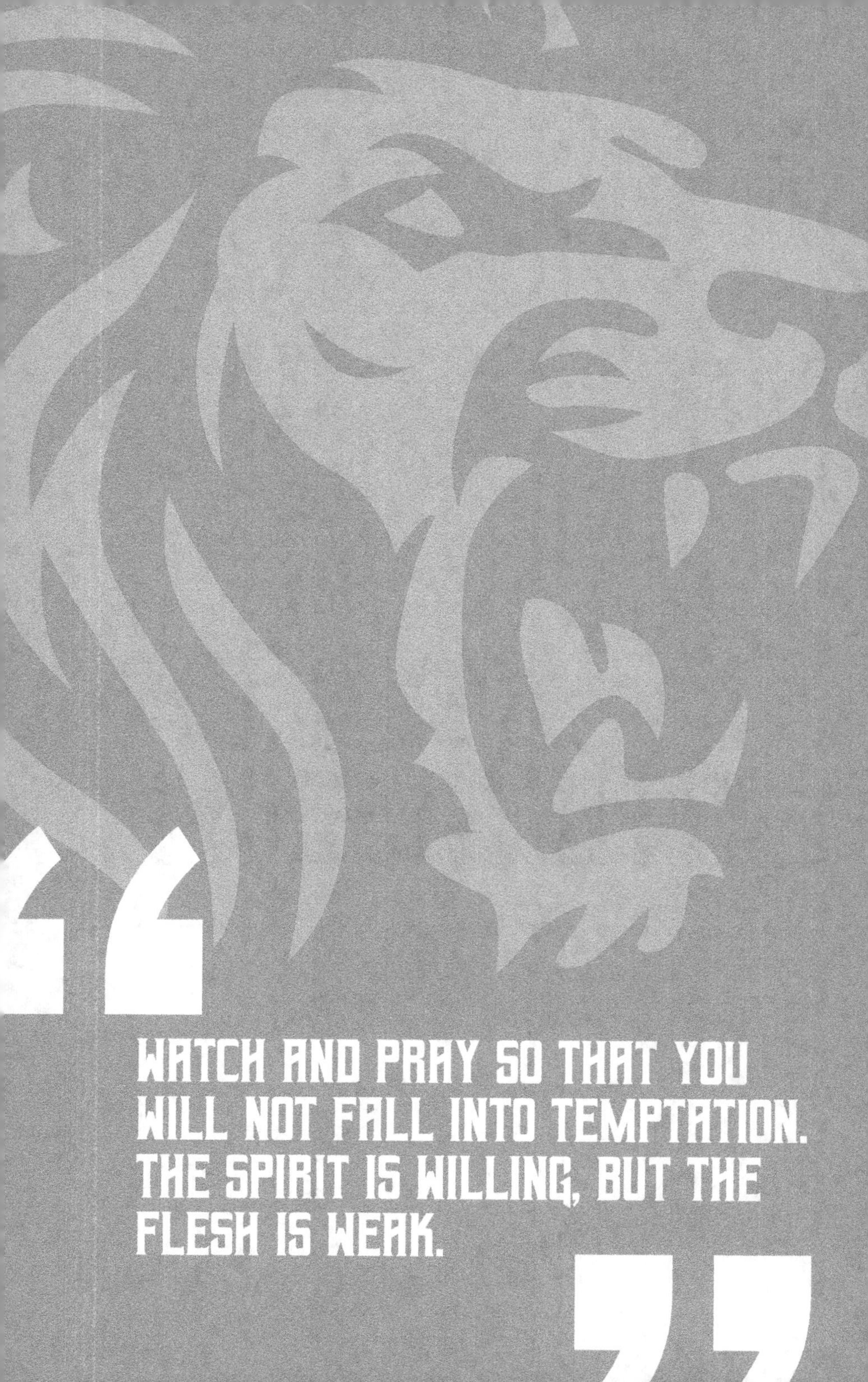
"
WATCH AND PRAY SO THAT YOU
WILL NOT FALL INTO TEMPTATION.
THE SPIRIT IS WILLING, BUT THE
FLESH IS WEAK.
"

CHAPTER 4

A LIONAWARENESS MINDSET

The first thing I noticed was the sound. In Hwange National Park, the air carries everything, wind through mopane leaves, the chunky rhythm of distant elephants, a birdcall I couldn't name. Our guide lifted two fingers and we froze. The grass ahead rose to our waists, the footpath narrowing to a thread. He whispered, "Eyes up. Stay close." So we did, heels quiet, breath measured, senses awake. Out there, **every step is an act of attention**, and **staying near the one who knows the land isn't optional; it's survival.**

That day branded into me what Scripture had already been teaching: spiritual life is not best lived on autopilot. It's lived awake, close to the Guide, with a calm, trained readiness. Peter's words feel like that guide's whisper: **"Be alert and of sober mind. Your enemy the devil prowls around like a roaring lion looking for someone to devour."** (1 Peter 5:8, NIV) Notice the posture he sketches in the surrounding verses, **humble yourselves under God's mighty hand** (v. 6), **cast all your anxiety on him because he cares for you** (v. 7), **resist him, standing firm in the faith** (vv. 8–9), and **expect restoration** after "a little while" (v. 10). Put together, it's a way of being: **eyes open, heart at rest, feet ready.**

What lionawareness is (and what it isn't)

The New Testament refuses to confuse anxiety with holiness. Paul writes, **"So then, let us not be like others, who are asleep, but let** us be awake and sober." (1 Thessalonians 5:6, NIV) He adds, **"Be very careful, then, how you live, not as unwise but as wise, making the most of every opportunity."** (Ephesians 5:15–16, NIV) And again, **"Devote yourselves to prayer, being watchful and thankful."** (Colossians 4:2, NIV) These lines don't conscript us as jittery sentries; they invite us to **live awake because we are loved and called.**

Two ditches to avoid:

- **Hypervigilance** baptizes worry as discernment, reading demons into delays and mistaking noise for wisdom.
- **Casual inattentiveness** baptizes distraction as "balance", calling drift "margin," ignoring the Shepherd's voice, and acting surprised when temptation arrives.

Jesus threads the needle: **"Watch and pray so that you will not fall into temptation. The spirit is willing, but the flesh is weak."** (Matthew 26:41, NIV) That's the stance, **alertness with dependence**, that keeps courage cleareyed instead of clenchedjawed. **Sober awareness is not fear; it is love that stays awake.**

Nehemiah's pattern: pray and post the guard

When enemies circled Jerusalem, Nehemiah didn't choose between spirituality and strategy. He records, **"We prayed to our God and posted a guard day and night to meet this threat."** (Nehemiah 4:9, NIV) A few lines later: the workers **"did their work with one hand and held a weapon in the other."** (Nehemiah 4:17, NIV) Prayer didn't replace preparation; **prayer powered preparation**. That is lionawareness in a sentence: we entrust the outcome to God and take responsibility for our part.

The inner mechanics of awareness

Peter's words carry practical weight. To "be alert" (*gregoreō*) is to stay awake when others doze; to be "sober" (*nēphō*) is to think clearly when others are fogged. Translate that into Tuesday:

- **Attention,** What has my eyes and ears?
- **Interpretation,** What am I actually looking at, temptation, fatigue, opportunity?
- **Intention,** Given that reality, what's my next faithful step?

Awareness without interpretation breeds anxiety; interpretation without intention breeds apathy. Awareness that moves toward wise action forms resilience.

The tall grasses where awareness earns its keep

Most ambushes don't arrive as spectacle; they hide in ordinary places. One of the most vulnerable moments is a **transition** after a win, in a loss, or when routines shift. Elijah's post-victory collapse shows how quickly strength can drain when the adrenaline fades; God met him there with rest, food, presence, and perspective (1 Kings 19). Ambushes also thrive in **isolation pockets** late nights, travel weeks, and unstructured hours when our guard is down, and our habits loosen. Scripture calls us out of that danger zone: "Let us consider how we may spur one another on… not giving up meeting together… but encouraging one another." (Hebrews 10:24–25, NIV)

There is a similar danger in the quiet drip of **screens and streams,** where constant inputs slowly shape the imagination. Paul's grid still holds true: "Whatever is true, whatever is noble, whatever is right, whatever is pure… think about such things." (Philippians 4:8, NIV) And then there are the **unresolved tensions** and bitterness that harden into a lens through which we view people and events. Hebrews warns us to "see to it… that no bitter root grows up to cause trouble and defile many." (Hebrews 12:15, NIV)

Lion awareness means pre-deciding how you'll move through these tall grasses, choosing your path before you feel the pull.

A simple rule of life (a trellis for love)

Small, durable rhythms beat occasional heroic efforts. Most of the Christian life isn't lived at the mountaintop but in the ordinary patterns that either drift us to sleep or keep us awake to God. A rule of life gives those ordinary moments structure, a trellis sturdy enough to support real growth. These small choices either dull us or awaken us. The 4 M's give us a simple framework to stay alert where it matters most.

Daily rhythms, the 4 M's (Morning, Mealtimes, Media, Margin)

Morning, Word before world. Before notifications and news, open Scripture and pray. Start low (humility), open (casting cares), alert (asking for awake eyes). **"Let the morning bring me word of your unfailing love, for I have put my trust in you."** (Psalm 143:8, NIV)

Mealtimes, turn tables into altars. Ask, "Where did you see God at work today?" **"Impress [these words] on your children... when you sit at home and when you walk along the road."** (Deuteronomy 6:7, NIV)

Media, curate on purpose. Replace endless scrolls with anchored reads. **"Be transformed by the renewing of your mind."** (Romans 12:2, NIV)

Margin, schedule breath. A five-minute mid-afternoon walk to pray **Matthew 26:41** keeps watchfulness from curdling into worry.

Weekly rhythms, the 4 A's (Assemble, Abide, Account, Active mercy)

Daily rhythms steady our footing, but awareness also grows in the patterns we keep over the course of a week. These weekly practices anchor us in community, rest, accountability, and mission, the places where spiritual strength deepens, and our lives stay aligned with the Shepherd's pace. Here are the 4 A's that shape a watchful, grounded week.

Assemble for worship. **"Not giving up meeting together... but encouraging one another."** (Hebrews 10:25, NIV) Gathered worship retrains your loves.

Abide in unhurried Sabbath. Refuse to live as if your worth rides on output. **"In repentance and rest is your salvation, in quietness and trust is your strength."** (Isaiah 30:15, NIV)

Account for your soul with an ally. Share temptations, victories, and next steps. **"Confess your sins to each other and pray for each other so that you may be healed."** (James 5:16, NIV)

Active mercy. Serve someone. Lionawareness is not navel-gazing; it is **love that watches and moves. "Let us consider how we may spur one another on toward love and good deeds."** (Hebrews 10:24, NIV)

Monthly rhythms, the 4 R's (Review, Repent, Reorder, Remember)

As weekly rhythms begin to steady your steps, monthly rhythms help you lift your eyes and take stock. These slower, wider practices create space to notice patterns, celebrate progress, and make small course corrections. That's where the 4 R's come in.

Review patterns, where did drift try to start? **"We must pay the most careful attention... so that we do not drift away."** (Hebrews 2:1, NIV)

Repent quickly and joyfully. **"If we confess our sins, he is faithful and just and will forgive us... and purify us."** (1 John 1:9, NIV)

Reorder your calendar to reflect your calling. **"Make the most of every opportunity."** (Ephesians 5:16, NIV)

Remember God's faithfulness, record answers to prayer. **"Praise the Lord... and forget not all his benefits."** (Psalm 103:2, NIV)

When vigilance masquerades as virtue

Some of us equate exhaustion with holiness, tight shoulders, clenched jaw, a dozen halffinished alarms inside the soul. But **"the**

Spirit God gave us does not make us timid, but gives us power, love and selfdiscipline." (2 Timothy 1:7, NIV) True lionawareness actually **calms** you because you're **clear**: you can name what's happening, and you know where to run.

Others equate good intentions with wisdom. "I'll be more careful," we say, but we never edit inputs, enlist allies, or change our pace. Daniel shows vigilance under pressure: windows open toward Jerusalem, prayer times intact, identity unbent (Daniel 6). Faithfulness looked like **staying predictable in holy ways**.

Training your senses (simple, repeatable drills)

One of the simplest ways to train your senses is to **watch your attention**. When you notice yourself doom-scrolling or spiraling inward, let that moment become a prayer: "Turn my eyes away from worthless things." (Psalm 119:37, NIV) Put the phone down, pick up the Word, or step outside and name three of God's kindnesses aloud. Small shifts in attention can reroute an entire day.

It also helps to **watch your language**, because words reveal drift. When "I'm on my own" rises in your heart, replace it with the truth: "The Lord is my shepherd." (Psalm 23:1, NIV) When you catch yourself saying, "I'll never change," answer with Scripture: "If anyone is in Christ, the new creation has come." (2 Corinthians 5:17, NIV) What you speak shapes what you believe, and what you believe shapes how you stand.

Then **watch your time**. Our hours flow in the direction of our loves, so put on your calendar what you claim to care about. Scripture urges us: "The night is nearly over; the day is almost here... clothe yourselves with the Lord Jesus Christ." (Romans 13:12, 14, NIV) Intentional time becomes a shield against drift.

Next, **watch your companions**, because proximity shapes possibility. As Proverbs reminds us, "Walk with the wise and become wise." (Proverbs 13:20, NIV) The people closest to you will either dull your awareness or deepen it.

And finally, **watch your doorways,** the predictable places where temptation knocks. Name the two contexts where you most often stumble, whether late-night isolation or travel-week loneliness, and write a "when this, then that" response now. Pre-decisions turn "I'll try" into "I already chose," and that simple clarity often closes the very door the enemy loves to crack open.

Case windows: where awareness changed the outcome

Here's what lion-awareness looks like in real life: ordinary people changing small patterns that had been quietly eroding their strength.

A young dad and his phone. Evenings were slipping into scrolling. He moved the phone to a kitchen charger at 6:30 p.m., opened a psalm before breakfast, and took a ten-minute night walk with his wife, asking, "Where did you see God today?" Attention followed intention; irritation dropped; patience rose.

A leader on the road. Hotel loneliness used to be a trap. Now the calendar carries counters: a pre-trip text to two allies, a Scripture card on the nightstand, and scheduled FaceTimes that make secrecy inconvenient. Practicing **"submit... then... resist"** (James 4:7, NIV) gave resistance teeth.

A student in a comparison spiral. She muted certain accounts, memorized **"A person can receive only what is given them from heaven."** (John 3:27, NIV), and served weekly with the kids' team. Inputs, identity, and mission realigned; joy returned.

Family watchfulness (not a bunker, a household)

If a predator were loose, your family would agree on doors, routes, and check-ins. Spiritually, that becomes **Word before world**, weekly worship as a non-negotiable, table talk ("Where did you see God at work today?"), confession and forgiveness practiced at home, and screen boundaries by conviction, not convenience. These aren't fear moves; they're **love operating like a watchman on the wall.** "We **prayed... and posted a guard."** (Nehemiah 4:9, NIV)

Why this matters for the mission

People who live awake love better. Because you're not numbed by noise, you notice needs. Because you're not ruled by hurry, you make time to bless. Because you're not duped by "angeloflight" offers, you keep truth and compassion together. Paul's compact charge holds it: **"Be on your guard; stand firm in the faith; be courageous; be strong. Do everything in love."** (1 Corinthians 16:13–14, NIV)

Field Drill (this week)

- **Two-minute morning liturgy:** Kneel if you can. Pray through 1 Peter 5:6–10, humble, cast, alert, resist, hope. Ask, "Lord, give me **clear eyes and a quiet heart** today."
- **Ruleoflife card:** Write the 4 M's (Morning, Mealtimes, Media, Margin). Circle one small change for each. Tape the card by your coffee.
- **Pre-decision list (two doorways):** Name the two settings where you most often stumble. Write your predetermined response (who you text, what you pray, what you replace the habit with).
- **Ally check:** Schedule two fiveminute calls with a trusted friend. Share your card; ask for theirs. **"Carry each other's burdens...."** (Galatians 6:2, NIV)

REFLECTION & APPLICATION

- Which ditch pulls you more, hypervigilance or casual inattentiveness, and why?

- Of the 4 M's and 4 A's, which single adjustment would most immediately steady your week?

- Where is your calendar out of alignment with your calling, and what small reorder will you make this month?

- Who will be your "posted guard", the person who gets your "ground is tilting" text, and when will you invite them?

Out on that Zimbabwe path, we didn't whiteknuckle our way through the bush; we stayed near the one who knew the terrain. That is lionawareness in a sentence. **The point isn't to study the grass until you're afraid; it's to stay close to the Guide until you're steady.** And as you walk, eyes up, heart at rest, let David's confession set the cadence of your stride: **"The Lord is my shepherd... Even though I walk through the darkest valley, I will fear no evil, for you are with me."** (Psalm 23:1, 4, NIV)

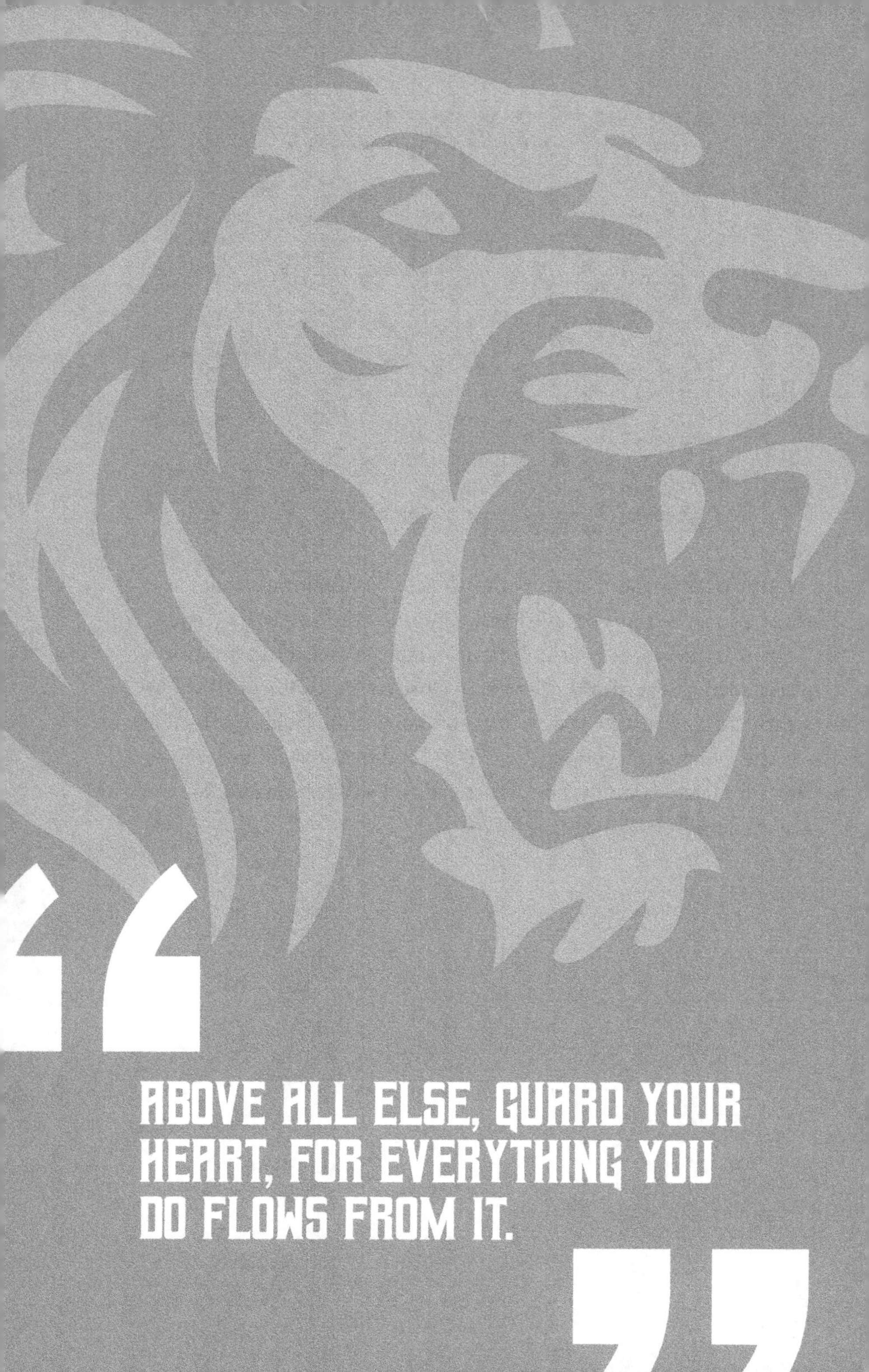

"
ABOVE ALL ELSE, GUARD YOUR HEART, FOR EVERYTHING YOU DO FLOWS FROM IT.
"

CHAPTER 5

GUARDING YOUR WEAK SPOTS

The fence looked solid, fresh boards, sturdy posts, everything straight as a sermon outline. Then hurricane season arrived. One afternoon the wind found a spot they had missed: a small side-gate latch they hadn't tightened. That little gap turned the whole gate into a sail. By morning, half the paneling was gone and the posts had started to lean. It wasn't the storm's size that surprised them; it was how such a **small** weakness gave the storm leverage. Spiritually, the same thing happens: **the enemy doesn't need a wide-open door, he only needs an unguarded one.**

You already feel the parallel. A pattern you "manage," a boundary you "bend," a habit you "don't have time" to address, tiny gaps that become entry points. Scripture keeps the warning simple and surgical: **"Above all else, guard your heart, for everything you do flows from it."** (Proverbs 4:23, NIV) Guarding isn't paranoia; it's discipleship. It's love planning ahead.

Why weak spots matter (and why they're easy to ignore)

Weak spots rarely announce themselves with sirens; they hide inside what feels normal. Pride slips in dressed as competence: "I've got this." Lust disguises itself as stress relief: "I deserve a break." Anger presents as honesty, even though the sharpness has nothing to do with truth. Hurry gets praised as productivity, even when it's thinning the soul. Isolation wears the mask of introversion, when in reality it's avoidance in disguise. And then there are the quieter distortions: approval, control, comfort, good desires swollen just out of place until they start acting like gods. These are the subtle openings the enemy looks for, the small latches that give the wind leverage.

James describes the physics of this drift with unnerving clarity: **"Each person is tempted when they are dragged away by their own evil desire and enticed. Then, after desire has conceived, it gives birth to sin; and sin, when it is fullgrown, gives birth to death."** (James 1:14–15, NIV) Notice the progression: desire → deception → decision → damage. **Sin rarely starts loud; it starts logical.**

Paul adds the countermove: **"Do not give the devil a foothold."** (Ephesians 4:27, NIV) A foothold is a place to push from. Weak spots are exactly that.

A few years ago, I sat across from a man in our church who loved Jesus deeply but felt completely defeated. He told me, "I don't know when it happened, but somewhere along the way I lost my footing." Nothing dramatic had taken him out, no scandal, no explosion, just a subtle pattern that grew roots. He had started staying up a little later. Then a little later than that. What began as "just unwinding" became scrolling, then isolation, then compromise, then shame. He said, "I didn't fall in a moment. I faded in small decisions I never challenged."

We traced the pattern backward together, and it was astonishing how clear it became once it was named. His weak spot wasn't the late-night hour itself, it was how predictable and unguarded it had become. But the turning point came not when he tried harder, but when he told the truth. He invited two trusted friends into the struggle, set a simple boundary, and practiced the submit → resist → replace rhythm each night before bed. Weeks later, he said something I'll never forget: "The moment I named my weak spot, it stopped feeling like a destiny and started feeling like a fight I could win." Sometimes victory begins with nothing more dramatic than honesty, light, and a small plan.

David shows how unguarded moments multiply. The story opens with one understated line: **"In the spring, at the time when kings go off to war... David remained in Jerusalem."** (2 Samuel 11:1, NIV) Wrong place, wrong time, unguarded heart. A glance becomes a look, a look becomes a message, and a message becomes a coverup. The man after God's heart didn't fall in a day; he fell in a series of **unresisted** steps.

Joseph models the other path. Cornered by Potiphar's wife, he answers with clarity and flight: **"How then could I do such a wicked thing and sin against God?"** (Genesis 39:9, NIV)... and when the pressure spikes, **"he left his cloak in her hand and ran out of the house."** (Genesis 39:12, NIV) Joseph didn't trust the room; he trusted God, and **he predecided to run**. Both stories teach the same lesson: **what you tolerate becomes what trains you.**

A "WeakSpot Audit" (name the gap before the wind finds it)

Use these questions this week. Be candid; the audit is grace, not guilt.

1. Patterns: When am I most vulnerable, late nights, travel weeks, conflict hangovers, victory letdowns?

2. People: Who amplifies temptation? Who helps me walk in the light?

3. Places & paths: Which rooms, routes, websites, or apps predict compromise?

4. Pressures: What feelings (lonely, angry, tired, bored) cue old escapes?

5. Permissions: What sentences do I use to excuse myself ("It's not that big a deal," "I deserve this," "I can stop later")?

If I can name the cue, I can change the course.

Pair the audit with a prayer: "Search me, God... see if there is any offensive way in me." **(Psalm 139:23–24, NIV)**

Build your guard plan (submit → resist → replace)

Awareness doesn't help much unless it leads to action. Scripture gives us a simple, repeatable pattern you've already seen, and now we'll apply it specifically to your weak spots.

We've been practicing the sequence in earlier chapters because Scripture insists on it:

- **Submit: "Submit yourselves, then, to God."** (James 4:7, NIV) Alignment first, His will over my wants.
- **Resist: "...Resist the devil, and he will flee from you."** (James 4:7, NIV) Say no in Jesus' name to the specific lure.
- **Replace**: Swap the habit's slot with a holy alternative (Word, prayer, text an ally, serve, step outside and give thanks). **If you don't replace, you'll replay.**

God promises real help in the moment: **"No temptation has overtaken you except what is common to mankind... he will also provide a way out so that you can endure it."** (1 Corinthians 10:13, NIV) Look for the exit **before** the elevator doors close.

Five common weak spots (and how grace trains new reflexes)

While weak spots vary from person to person, these five show up again and again in the lives of believers. Naming them helps us recognize patterns before they become pitfalls.

1) Pride (selfreliance).

Symptom: low prayer, low input from others. Quiet belief: *I'm the exception.*

Counter: Start low daily. **"God opposes the proud but shows favor to the humble."** (1 Peter 5:5, NIV) Ask for counsel **before** decisions. Keep a running list of "I was wrong" moments; let them become worship, not humiliation.

2) Lust (secret escape).

Symptom: secrecy, shameseesaw, tech patterns at predictable hours.

Counter: Predecide your device rules (charging location, filters, time windows). Confess fast and in the light: **"Confess your sins to each other and pray for each other so that you may be healed."** (James 5:16, NIV) Replace the trigger with embodied praise: memorize **"I made a covenant with my eyes."** (Job 31:1, NIV) and go for a fiveminute gratitude walk.

3) Anger (stored hurts).

Symptom: simmering sarcasm, short fuse, reheated arguments in your head.

Counter: Slow your words, speed your forgiveness. **"Everyone should be quick to listen, slow to speak and slow to become angry."** (James 1:19, NIV) Name the wound with a mature believer; practice blessing the person you resent (Luke 6:28).

4) Hurry (thin soul).

Symptom: no margin, constant distraction, dulled compassion.

Counter: Sabbath without apology. Anchor morning and mealtimes. **"Be very careful, then, how you live, not as unwise but as wise...."** (Ephesians 5:15–16, NIV) Put Scripture before screens, especially on heavy days.

5) Isolation (solo fight).

Symptom: canceled checkins, "I'm fine," but you're not.

Counter: Reenter a small group, and appoint two allies who can ask anything, anytime. **"Though one may be overpowered, two can defend themselves. A cord of three strands is not quickly broken."** (Ecclesiastes 4:12, NIV)

Thought warfare (close the inside gate)

The battle is won or lost where thoughts live. Paul's counsel is an action plan: **"We demolish arguments and every pretension that sets itself up against the knowledge of God, and we take captive every thought to make it obedient to Christ."** (2 Corinthians 10:5, NIV)

Try this threeline drill when a thought presses:

- **Name it**: Is this accusation, comparison, fantasy, or fear?
- **Narrate it**: "This thought leads me away from Jesus by _______."
- **Neutralize it**: Answer with the Word: fear → **"The Lord is my light and my salvation, whom shall I fear?"** (Psalm 27:1, NIV); shame → **"There is now no condemnation..."** (Romans 8:1, NIV); temptation → **"[He] will... provide a way out."** (1 Corinthians 10:13, NIV)

You can't starve a lie by staring at it; you starve it by feeding on truth.

Boundaries are not legalism; they're love

When Jesus talks radically about removing what causes you to stumble (Matthew 5:29–30), He is not commending selfharm; He is commending **seriousness**. Paul says it this way: **"Clothe yourselves with the Lord Jesus Christ, and do not think about how to gratify the desires of the flesh."** (Romans 13:14, NIV)

So write **predecisions** in plain language:

- **If** I am alone in a hotel after 9 p.m., **then** I will call an ally and leave the TV off.
- **If** I feel the comparison spiral, **then** I will log off for 24 hours and text one encouragement to someone I'm tempted to resent.
- **If** we fight at home, **then** after a tenminute cooldown I will ask, "What am I not hearing?" and pray out loud for both of us.

"The prudent see danger and take refuge." (Proverbs 27:12, NIV) Boundaries don't mean you're weak; they mean you're wise.

Train with the Spirit, not just for the Spirit

Whiteknuckling never lasts. Paul's invitation is relational: **"So I say, walk by the Spirit, and you will not gratify the desires of the flesh."**

(Galatians 5:16, NIV) Ask the Spirit each morning: "Where am I likely to be tempted today? What would faithfulness look like in that moment?" Then listen for His prompts, He often warns quietly **before** the pressure shouts.

Pair this with hope: **"Let us throw off everything that hinders and the sin that so easily entangles."** (Hebrews 12:1, NIV) Throwing off is not a onetime drama; it's a daily, cheerful refusal.

Case windows (composites from pastoral life)

The latenight scroll. Stressful day, spouse asleep, phone glow. The new plan put the charger in the kitchen, set a 9:30 "screens down" alarm, and added a short Psalm aloud before bed. Within two weeks, sleep improved and shame cycles shrank.

The roadwarrior leader. Hotels had become haunted. Pretrip texts went to two allies, a Scripture card sat by the keycard, and FaceTime calls filled the loneliest hour. The room didn't change; the rules did.

The quietly resentful parent. Hidden scorekeeping was poisoning tenderness. They started a "fast forgiveness" practice: pray blessing for the person who hurt you within 24 hours and schedule a calm conversation. Anger lost oxygen; affection returned.

In each story, victory didn't come from a heroic moment; it came from **humble, repeatable moves** done in the light.

When you slip (because sometimes you will)

David's prayer isn't theory; it's a roadmap back: **"Have mercy on me, O God... Create in me a pure heart... Restore to me the joy of your salvation."** (Psalm 51:1, 10, 12, NIV) Run toward God, not away. Confess specifically, receive cleansing, and reengage your predecisions. Remember: **"There is now no condemnation for those who are in Christ Jesus."** (Romans 8:1, NIV) **Grace doesn't excuse sin; grace equips you to stand up and walk again.**

Field Drill (this week)

- **Do the WeakSpot Audit.** Write your answers, not just think them. Circle the top **two** weak spots that most often open the gate.

- **Predecision sheet.** For each weak spot, write one **if/then** plan you'll follow for 30 days. Put the sheet on your nightstand.

- **Twoally text.** Ask two believers to be on call this month. Give them permission to ask anything, anytime. **"Carry each other's burdens...."** (Galatians 6:2, NIV)

- **Truth card.** Choose three verses (fear, identity, temptation). Keep them on your lock screen and speak them aloud in the moment.

- **HALT check.** Twice a day ask, "Am I Hungry, Angry, Lonely, or Tired?" If yes, address the body and the soul before making decisions.

REFLECTION & APPLICATION

- Which "small latch" in your life has given the wind leverage lately, pride, lust, anger, hurry, isolation, or something else?

- What **if/then** predecision will you write today, and who will you share it with?

- Where do you need to trade secrecy for light (James 5:16), and what will your first sentence be when you reach out?

- How will you practice **submit** → **resist** → **replace** in the next 48 hours?

You don't strengthen a fence by wishing the wind away; you strengthen it by **tightening the places that give the wind a hold**. Spiritually, the same is true. Identify the gap, invite the Spirit, involve your people, and obey in small, stubborn ways. **Sin may be crouching at the door,** Scripture says so (Genesis 4:7, NIV), but so is grace, and **grace trains you to say "no"** and to live awake (Titus 2:11–12, NIV). Guard your weak spots, and watch how joy returns.

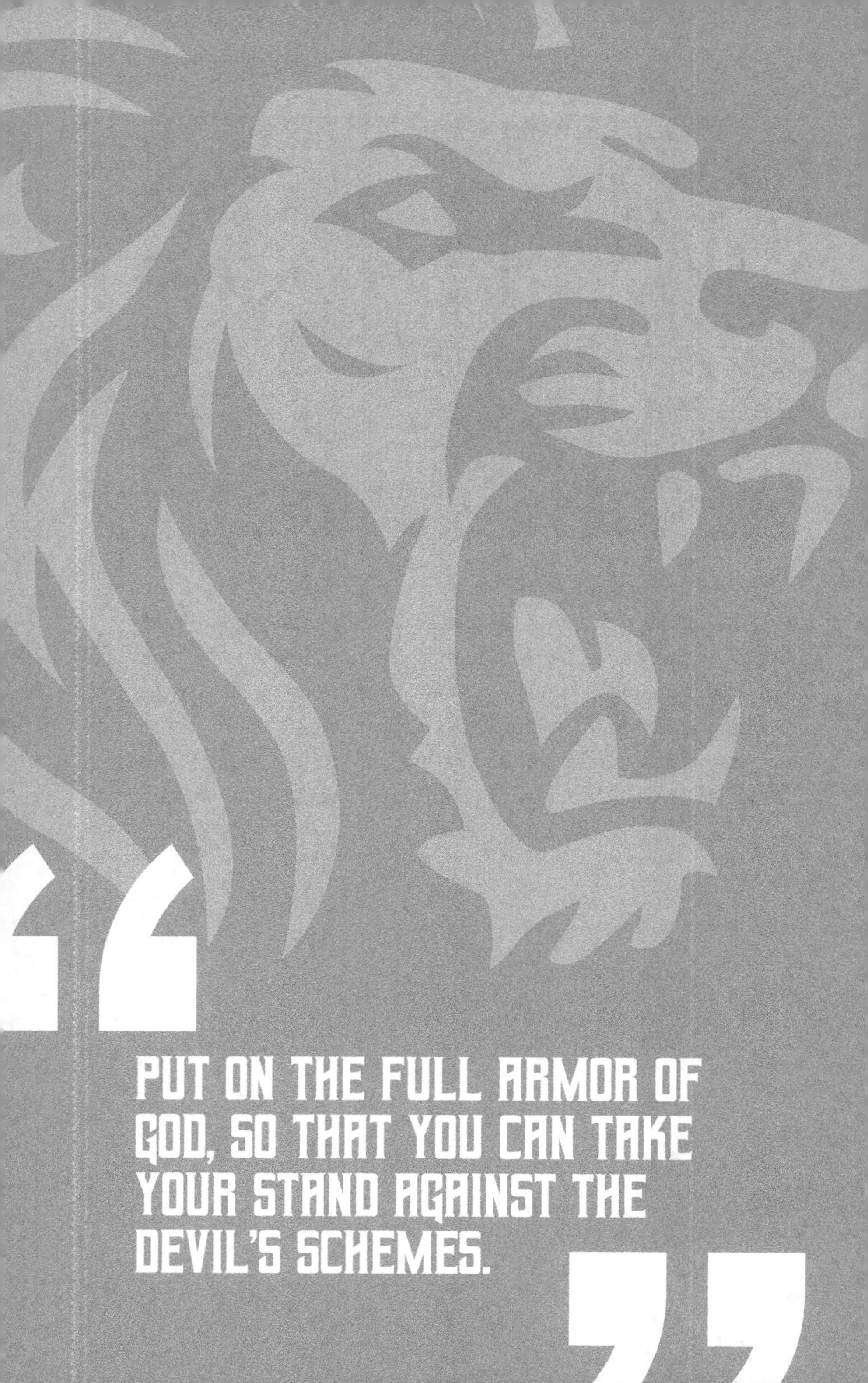

"
PUT ON THE FULL ARMOR OF GOD, SO THAT YOU CAN TAKE YOUR STAND AGAINST THE DEVIL'S SCHEMES.
"

CHAPTER 6

ARMING YOURSELF FOR BATTLE

I grew up on Army posts where cadence rolled like thunder at dawn. Before a mission or march, soldiers lined up for inspection, boots laced, webbing tight, each piece of gear checked and rechecked because in the field, **small misses become big losses.** Nobody wandered into a fight wondering where their helmet was. You geared up on purpose, before the first step. That picture has never left me, and when I read Paul's words in Ephesians 6, it feels like standing on a parade field again, hearing the call to be ready.

Paul begins with where the strength actually comes from: **"Finally, be strong in the Lord and in his mighty power." (Ephesians 6:10, NIV)** The command isn't "be strong in yourself"; it's **be strengthened** by the Lord. Then the order: **"Put on the full armor of God, so that you can take your stand against the devil's schemes." (Ephesians 6:11, NIV)** This is not hobby gear; this is survival gear, because **"our struggle is not against flesh and blood"** but against spiritual forces we cannot see. **(Ephesians 6:12, NIV)**

Here's the promise tucked inside the charge: **"Put on the full armor of God, so that when the day of evil comes, you may be able to stand your ground... and after you have done everything, to stand." (Ephesians 6:13, NIV)** Notice the repetition, **stand.** In Christ, the goal is not panic; it is perseverance.

Because the battle is real and your strength isn't, **armor is not decoration; it's daily dependence.**

The Belt of Truth, holding everything together

Paul starts with the belt because a soldier's belt anchored every other piece. Truth does that for the soul. **"Stand firm then, with the belt of truth buckled around your waist." (Ephesians 6:14, NIV)** In a world where lies trend and halftruths masquerade as compassion, truth keeps the whole life from sagging.

Practically, this is both **doctrinal** and **daily**. Doctrinally, you anchor in what God has revealed, who God is, who you are, what sin and salvation are. Daily, you refuse to let feelings or headlines outrank Scripture. Jesus promised, **"Then you will know the truth, and the truth will set you free." (John 8:32, NIV)** Freedom isn't the absence of limits; it's the presence of truth.

How to buckle it on today: build a simple **truth inventory**. When pressure rises, ask, "What is true about God here? What is true about me in Christ? What is true about this temptation?" Then answer with Scripture you can say aloud. **Truth spoken becomes courage strengthened.**

Truth secures the center, but the heart still needs protection. That's why Paul moves next to the breastplate.

The Breastplate of Righteousness, guarding the vital center

The breastplate covers the heart and lungs, the core. **"With the breastplate of righteousness in place." (Ephesians 6:14, NIV)** There's a double edge here:

- **Imputed righteousness**, you're covered by Christ's perfect record. **"God made him who had no sin to be sin for us... so that in him we might become the righteousness of God." (2 Corinthians 5:21, NIV)** This is your **position**; accusation can't pierce it.
- **Practiced righteousness**, you choose the way that fits your new life. **"Above all else, guard your heart, for everything you do flows from it." (Proverbs 4:23, NIV)** This is your

practice; compromise can't carve you open if you don't unbuckle the plate.

How to wear it: keep a **short list** with God and people. Confess fast, forgive fast. When shame hisses, answer with your position (**Romans 8:1**) and take a step in righteousness today (call back, make it right, delete the thread). **Righteousness protects you from both pride and despair.**

Once the heart is guarded, the next question is: where are you walking? That's the wisdom of the gospel shoes.

Shoes of the Gospel of Peace, footing in a shaken world

In battle, footing is everything. **"With your feet fitted with the readiness that comes from the gospel of peace." (Ephesians 6:15, NIV)** The gospel gives you **grip**, peace with God through Christ (objective), and the peace of God in your spirit (felt). When anxiety or chaos tries to slide you, the gospel holds you steady.

How to lace them up: preach to yourself in moments of swirl: *Because of Jesus, I am reconciled to God; I am not walking into this alone.* Then move toward peacemaking with people: **"If it is possible, as far as it depends on you, live at peace with everyone." (Romans 12:18, NIV)** You're not passive; you're ready. **Peace is not the absence of conflict; it's Christ's presence giving you traction.**

With a steady footing in the gospel, you're grounded, but grounded doesn't mean unopposed. Arrows still fly. Stability needs defense, which is why the next piece is the shield.

The Shield of Faith, quenching what burns

Ancient shields were large, layered, and often water-soaked, so flaming arrows sizzled out on impact. **"Take up the shield of faith, with which you can extinguish all the flaming arrows of the evil one." (Ephesians 6:16, NIV)** Arrows still fly, accusation, lust, cynicism, despair. Faith doesn't pretend they aren't coming. **Faith raises the shield, and they lose their fire.**

Faith is not a mood; it is trust in God's character and Word **right now. "Now faith is confidence in what we hope for and assurance about what we do not see." (Hebrews 11:1, NIV)**

How to lift it: answer each arrow with a **faith headline:**

- *Arrow:* "You're on your own." → *Shield:* **"Never will I leave you; never will I forsake you." (Hebrews 13:5, NIV)**
- *Arrow:* "You can't change." → *Shield:* **"If anyone is in Christ, the new creation has come." (2 Corinthians 5:17, NIV)**
- *Arrow:* "This will crush you." → *Shield:* **"My grace is sufficient for you, for my power is made perfect in weakness." (2 Corinthians 12:9, NIV)**

Faith doesn't remove the arrows; it extinguishes them.

And yet, even as the shield extinguishes what comes at you, the battle also rages in you, especially in the mind. A soldier might block the arrows and still lose the fight if his thoughts collapse. So, Paul lifts our attention to the helmet.

The Helmet of Salvation, guarding the mind with assurance

Helmets save lives because head wounds end fights. **"Take the helmet of salvation." (Ephesians 6:17, NIV)** The enemy loves mind games, doubt of God's goodness, fear about your future, and confusion about your identity. Assurance fortifies your thinking: **"Take captive every thought to make it obedient to Christ." (2 Corinthians 10:5, NIV)**

Assurance isn't arrogance; it's confidence in Christ's finished work. **"The one who is in you is greater than the one who is in the world." (1 John 4:4, NIV)**

How to strap it on: practice a daily **identity rehearsal.** Say aloud three gospel facts:

1. I am adopted: **"See what great love the Father has lavished on us, that we should be called children of God!" (1 John 3:1, NIV)**

2. I am forgiven: **"In him we have redemption... the forgiveness of sins." (Ephesians 1:7, NIV)**

3. I am secure: **"There is now no condemnation for those who are in Christ Jesus." (Romans 8:1, NIV)**

Assurance is oxygen for perseverance.

With your mind guarded by assurance, you're almost fully outfitted, but armor alone doesn't win battles. You need a weapon, not to wound people, but to silence lies. That weapon is the Word.

The Sword of the Spirit, Scripture on your tongue

This is the one offensive weapon in the list, and Paul clarifies what it is: **"the sword of the Spirit, which is the word of God." (Ephesians 6:17, NIV)** In the wilderness, Jesus met temptation with Scripture every time: **"It is written..." (Matthew 4:1–11, NIV)** He didn't negotiate with the tempter; He **answered** him.

How to carry it well:

- **Memorize small, use often.** Three verses for fear, identity, and temptation will do more than thirty you never recall.
- **Speak it out loud.** Scripture spoken interrupts spirals. **Scripture on your tongue turns panic into prayer.**
- **Apply, don't just admire.** The sword is for real moments; use it at 11:37 p.m., in the parking lot, in the meeting.

But even with every piece in place, there is something more that fills the armor with strength. The battle is not fought in spiritual silence; it is fought in prayer. Prayer is the atmosphere that animates every piece.

Prayer, the atmosphere of the armor

Paul doesn't stop with six pieces; he situates them in constant prayer: **"And pray in the Spirit on all occasions with all kinds of prayers and requests... be alert and always keep on praying for all the Lord's people." (Ephesians 6:18, NIV)** The armor doesn't replace prayer; prayer animates the armor. This is why the order we've been using matters so much: **"Submit yourselves, then, to God. Resist the** devil, and he will flee from you." (James 4:7, NIV) Stand under God before you stand against evil. Prayer is that submission in action.

A 90Second "SuitUp" Litany (for real mornings)

You don't put armor on once a year; you put it on before you step into the day. Here's a quick litany you can pray while the coffee drips:

- **Belt of Truth:** *Lord, fasten me to what is true. I will not let my feelings outrank Your Word.*
- **Breastplate of Righteousness:** *Thank You that I'm covered by Jesus. Help me act like who I already am.*
- **Gospel Shoes:** *Set my footing in Your peace. Make me a peacemaker where I walk today.*
- **Shield of Faith:** *I trust You to quench what burns. When lies fly, prompt me to raise the shield.*
- **Helmet of Salvation:** *Guard my mind in the assurance of Your finished work.*
- **Sword of the Spirit:** *Put Your Word on my tongue. Let me answer lies with what You have said.*
- **Prayer:** *I submit to You. Lead me; I will resist the evil one by Your power.*

Ninety seconds. Deep breath. Step forward.

Training vs. Trying

Soldiers don't "try harder" on game day; they **train daily** so that right moves become reflex. In the same way, set rhythms that keep you battleready:

- **Word before world** (Scripture before notifications).
- **Confession early** (don't carry sin to bedtime; 1 John 1:9).
- **Community weekly** (you need shields locked with yours; Hebrews 10:24–25).
- **Pre-decisions written** (if/then scripts for your two most common temptations).

- **Sabbath honestly** (rest is resistance to the tyranny of hurry; Isaiah 30:15).

You can't strap on armor in the middle of an ambush; you suit up before the fight finds you.

Case Windows (composites from pastoral life)

The late-night ambush. He'd say, "I'll be careful," and then stumble at 11 p.m. His shift wasn't superhuman resolve; it was **pre-decisions plus armor**: phone on the kitchen charger at 9:30, Psalm aloud at 10:00, a text to an ally when loneliness hit, and the **sword** ready with **1 Corinthians 10:13** on his lips. The arrows still flew; the **shield** started hissing them out.

The tense staff meeting. She walked in braced to defend herself. Forty minutes in, she sensed the slide, old narratives, quick offense. She silently prayed the litany: **peace for footing, truth for clarity, assurance for her mind**. Speaking slowly, she owned her part and blessed a critic. That day the **gospel shoes** kept her from skidding.

The anxious parent. A wave of what-ifs rose like a tide. Instead of doomscrolling, they took a ten-minute walk, practiced the identity rehearsal (child, forgiven, secure), and prayed by name for their son, **"casting all your anxiety on him because he cares for you." (1 Peter 5:7, NIV)** Worry didn't vanish; it lost the steering wheel.

Common Missteps (and how the armor answers them)

- **Moralism without Jesus:** Trying to behave better without resting in Christ's righteousness. *Answer:* **Breastplate**, you're covered by Jesus first, then you act like it.
- **Spiritualizing without Scripture:** Big feelings, little Bible. *Answer:* **Belt/Sword**, let God's Word define and defend.
- **Peacekeeping instead of peacemaking:** Avoidance to keep calm. *Answer:* **Gospel Shoes**, real peace moves toward truth in love.

- **Fighting people instead of lies:** Turning neighbors into enemies. *Answer:* **Helmet/Shield**, guard your thoughts; treat people like imagebearers; fight the arrows.

Field Drill (this week)

- **Write your SuitUp Litany** in your own words and tape it where you get ready. Pray it daily for seven days.
- **Truth inventory:** Choose one anxious or tempting moment each day. Write two sentences: "What's the lie? What's the Scripture answer?" Speak the answer aloud.
- **Predecisions:** Name your top two "ambush windows" (time/place). Create one if/then guardrail for each and share with an ally.
- **Shield practice:** Build your three "faith headlines" (verses you'll use for fear, identity, temptation). Make them your phone's lock screen for a week.
- **Prayer coverage:** Pick **two people** to pray for daily (Eph 6:18), one in your home, one at church. Text them midweek: "Praying Ephesians 6 over you today."

REFLECTION & APPLICATION

- Which piece of the armor do you instinctively neglect, and what is it costing you right now?

- Where does your footing slip most, conflict at work, latenight loneliness, family stress, and how will you lace up **gospel peace** there this week?

- What are your top two flaming arrows? Write your **faith headlines** to answer them and practice saying them out loud.

- Who needs your intercession and encouragement as they fight? How will you "keep on praying for all the Lord's people" **(Ephesians 6:18, NIV)** this week?

You don't march out to prove your strength; you **stand** in **His**. The enemy still schemes, but the cross still speaks. **"And having disarmed the powers and authorities, he made a public spectacle of them, triumphing over them by the cross." (Colossians 2:15, NIV)** So suit up, step out, and remember: **you don't fight for victory, you fight from it,** under the hand of the God who clothes His people in what they need and then walks with them into the field.

PART III
FIGHT TOGETHER

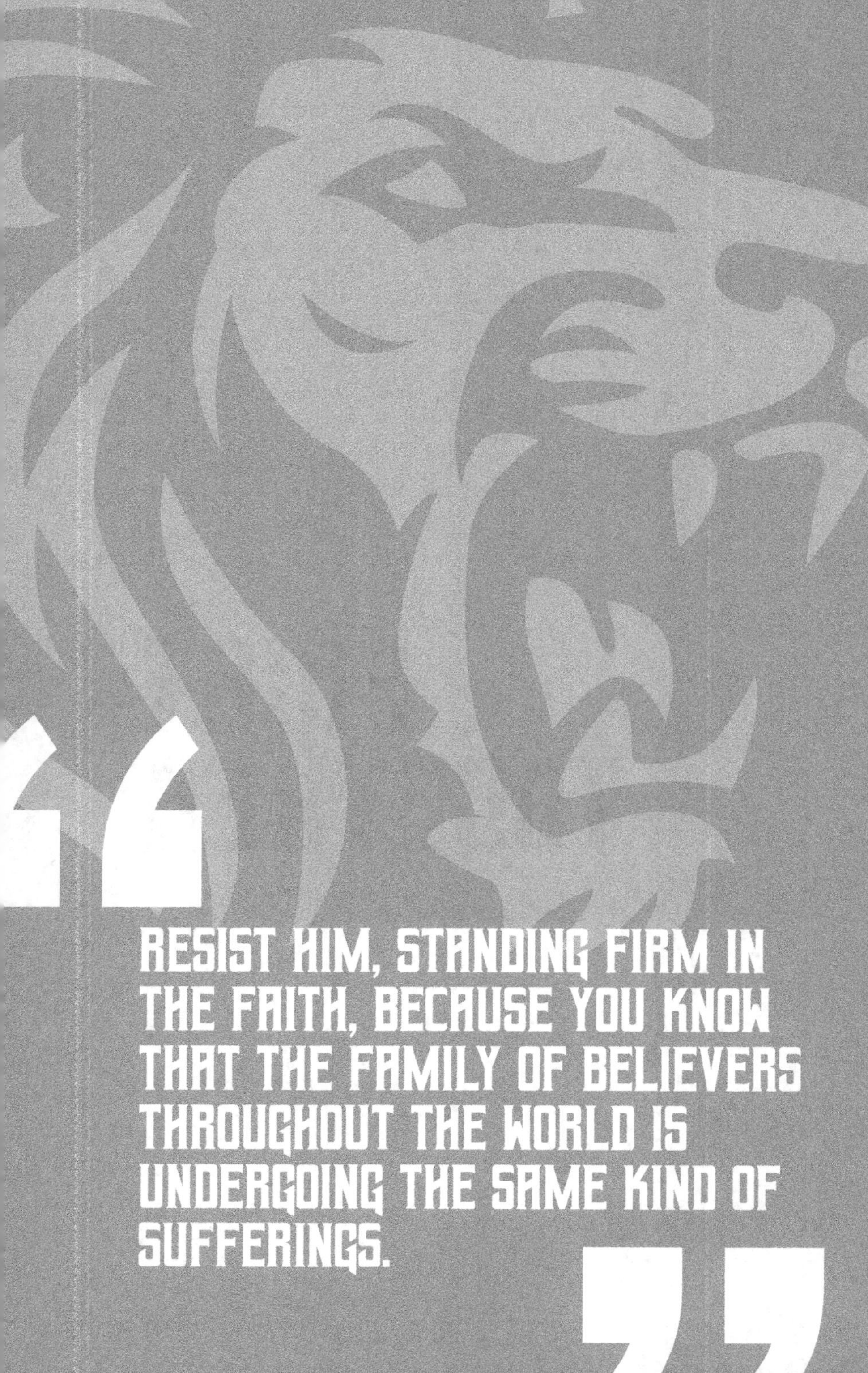
"
RESIST HIM, STANDING FIRM IN THE FAITH, BECAUSE YOU KNOW THAT THE FAMILY OF BELIEVERS THROUGHOUT THE WORLD IS UNDERGOING THE SAME KIND OF SUFFERINGS.
"

CHAPTER 7

THE DANGER OF ISOLATION

The text came late, "I'm good. Just need space."

Two weeks earlier we'd noticed the empty chair in our men's group. Work had been heavy, he said. Kids' schedules crazy. "I'll be back next month." Then came the quiet. The next time I saw him, he wasn't "good." He was tired, angry at himself, and surprised by how fast "space" had turned into secrecy. He said a sentence I've heard more times than I can count:

"I was fine... until I wasn't."

We prayed, we talked, and we traced the path backward. It didn't start with a scandal; it started with **isolation that felt reasonable**. And that's the trap. **Isolation promises relief; it produces vulnerability.**

The Scriptures are blunt about this. Peter lifts our eyes from our private worlds to a global family under fire and says, **"Resist him, standing firm in the faith, because you know that the family of believers throughout the world is undergoing the same kind of sufferings." (1 Peter 5:9, NIV)** Resistance is easier when you remember you're not the only one resisting. The enemy prowls; he also **preys on stragglers**. So this chapter is a rescue mission for anyone drifting to the edges and a training chapter for the rest of us to pull friends back to the center.

Why isolation feels attractive (and why it's a lie)

It sells itself as rest: *I just need a break.* Sometimes it masquerades as strength: *I'll handle this myself.* Often it hides behind a kind of protectiveness: *People won't understand; I'll only make it worse.* But Scripture keeps exposing the pattern. **Isolation distorts perspective.** Elijah believed he was the only faithful one left and wanted to quit. God met him with presence, provision, and the reminder that thousands had not bowed (1 Kings 19). When you're alone, the enemy's whisper starts to sound like your own voice.

Isolation weakens resistance. Jesus' simple instruction still diagnoses our need: "Watch and pray so that you will not fall into temptation. The spirit is willing, but the flesh is weak." (Matthew 26:41, NIV) When we're alone, watching grows thin and prayer grows quiet.

And **isolation turns embers cold.** The early church's pattern wasn't casual attendance but stubborn togetherness: "Let us consider how we may spur one another on toward love and good deeds, not giving up meeting together... but encouraging one another." (Hebrews 10:24–25, NIV) The ember that rolls away from the fire always loses heat; community is the hearth where courage stays hot.

Sin grows in silence; healing grows in the light. James puts it plainly: "Confess your sins to each other and pray for each other so that you may be healed." (James 5:16, NIV)

What isolation costs

Isolation carries a cost, and the first thing it steals is **clarity**. Alone, we misread motives, magnify slights, and minimize real danger. Proverbs reminds us, **"The way of fools seems right to them, but the wise listen to advice."** (Proverbs 12:15, NIV) When you're part of gospel community, you gain mirrors who reflect truth and mapmakers who help you see the path you're actually on.

Isolation also erodes **resilience**. Ecclesiastes keeps the math simple and the imagery strong: **"Two are better than one... If either** of them falls down, one can help the other up... Though one may be overpowered, two can defend themselves. A cord of three strands is not quickly broken." (Ecclesiastes 4:9–12, NIV) When your life is braided with others, you fray slower and stand stronger.

Then there's the cost to **joy**. When you pull back from the body of Christ, worship becomes optional, service feels heavy, and gratitude grows thin. The New Testament's "one anothers" are not niceties; they are conduits of joy, encouraging, carrying, forgiving, restoring (Romans 12; Galatians 6; 1 Thessalonians 5, NIV). Joy grows where lives intersect, not where they isolate.

And finally, isolation weakens your **protection**. Paul reminds us that our real struggle is not against flesh and blood (Ephesians 6:12), which means people aren't your enemy, but they are your shield wall. In the ancient world, shields were designed to lock together; no soldier fought alone. Strength multiplies when shoulders are close.

Seeing the cost should wake us up, but it still leaves an honest question: *If isolation is this damaging, why do we keep drifting toward it?* Scripture doesn't shame the struggle; it names the reasons with surprising clarity.

Why we withdraw (and what to put in its place)

We withdraw for reasons that feel understandable in the moment. Sometimes it's **exhaustion** that the pace becomes unsustainable, so we drop what seems optional: community. But community isn't optional fuel; it's an essential strength. The better move is to replace withdrawal with Sabbath honesty and smaller, steadier touchpoints. A ten-minute weekly check-in will serve your soul far better than a monthly hour you'll likely cancel. Scripture whispers the remedy: "In quietness and trust is your strength." (Isaiah 30:15, NIV)

Other times the driver is **shame**. We fail, and distance masquerades as humility. But hiding is not holiness. The gospel invites confession and covering, not self-punishment, but repentance and repair. "There is now no condemnation for those who are in Christ Jesus." (Romans 8:1, NIV) Healing begins where shame meets light.

Sometimes we withdraw because of **offense**. Someone hurts us, and retreat feels safer than reconciliation. But Jesus gives us a path forward in Matthew 18, and Paul calls us to Ephesians 4 meekness: "Be completely humble and gentle... bearing with one another in love." (Ephesians 4:2–3, NIV) Reconciliation is rarely quick, but it is always healthier than silent drifting.

And then there is **pride,** that quiet preference for independence over interdependence. Pride whispers, *I don't need anyone,* but the body of Christ tells a different story: "If one part suffers, every part suffers with it... you are the body of Christ." (1 Corinthians 12:26–27, NIV) Strength grows where lives interlock.

Finally, many of us withdraw because of **busyness**. We become overcommitted to good things and underconnected to the Best. Community gets squeezed out, not by sin, but by schedules. The countermove is intentionality, a rule of life that puts people on the calendar on purpose. Paul's reminder rings true: "Make the most of every opportunity." (Ephesians 5:16, NIV)

Independence feels strong; interdependence makes you strong.

Scripture gives us windows that pull us back from the edge. The first church "devoted themselves to the apostles' teaching and to fellowship, to the breaking of bread and to prayer." (Acts 2:42, NIV) Not dabbling devotion. The apostle Paul modeled this beautifully; though often imprisoned and isolated physically, he never wrote as a solo Christian. His letters are filled with names, co-workers, households, greetings, the gospel traveling across friendship lines. And over it all stands the Great Shepherd: "God sets the lonely in families." (Psalm 68:6, NIV) If loneliness has been your address, the church is meant to become your new street.

You need a real-time discerner when you're teetering toward the edges. In moments of pullback, ask:

- Does this voice **draw** me to Jesus with conviction and a next step, or **drive** me away with shame and finality?
- Does this voice move me **toward** the light with a person, or **deeper into** secrecy?

"My sheep listen to my voice; I know them, and they follow me." (John 10:27, NIV) The Shepherd's voice draws, the enemy's voice drives. When the difference is murky, hand the moment to Scripture and to a trusted believer and let the light do its work (Ephesians 5:13, NIV).

A 14-Day Re-Entry Plan (when you've been drifting)

Design: small, doable steps that rebuild reflexes, not pressure.

Day 1. Text the ally. "Ground is tilting, can we talk this week?" **"Carry each other's burdens." (Galatians 6:2, NIV)**

Day 2. Come to worship. Don't wait to "feel ready." Stand under the Word and among God's people. **(Hebrews 10:25, NIV)**

Day 3. Name the drift. Write three sentences: Where did it start? What made it "reasonable"? What did it cost? Pray **Psalm 139:23–24** (NIV).

Day 4. Rejoin a circle. Email or text your group leader. Put the next meeting on your calendar.

Day 5. One honest coffee. Share a specific struggle with a mature believer. Ask for prayer and one small assignment. **(James 5:16, NIV)**

Day 6. Serve someone. Deliver a meal, write a note, stack chairs at youth. Mission reorients. **(Hebrews 10:24, NIV)**

Day 7. Table talk. Ask at dinner, "Where did you see God today?" Normalize light at home. **(Deuteronomy 6:7, NIV)**

Day 8. Scripture aloud. Read a psalm out loud morning and night. Scripture on your tongue interrupts spirals. **(Psalm 119:105, NIV)**

Day 9. Predecision. Write one if/then boundary for your most tempting hour. Share it with your ally. **(Romans 13:14, NIV)**

Day 10. Pray for two others. Text them you're praying **Ephesians 6:18** (NIV). Your intercession strengthens you, too.

Day 11. Repair a small fracture. Make a call you've avoided. **"As far as it depends on you, live at peace." (Romans 12:18, NIV)**

Day 12. Schedule rest. A twohour block without screens. Walk, read, nap, delight. **(Isaiah 30:15, NIV)**

Day 13. Invite someone new in. Ask a couple or friend to your table this week. Hospitality fights hiding.

Day 14. Review & renew. Where did light break in? What needs another 14 days? Commit with your ally.

You don't drift back by accident; you return by arrangement.

Building your "Barnabas Circle" (three kinds of allies)

Of course, community isn't always easy. The very people God uses to heal us can also be the ones who unintentionally harm us. That's why we need wisdom for the moments when connection costs something.

Every believer needs a **Barnabas,** an encourager, someone who can see grace on your life when you can't see it yourself. Barnabas had that gift in the early church: "He was a good man, full of the Holy Spirit and faith." (Acts 11:24, NIV) This kind of friend lifts your chin when it drops and reminds you of who you are in Christ when circumstances try to tell you otherwise.

You also need a **Nathan,** a truth teller. Nathan was the one who could stand before King David and say, "You're the man," and David leaned in, not out (2 Samuel 12). Truth without love wounds, and love without truth withholds what you actually need. A Nathan brings both: courage and compassion, clarity and care.

And you need an **Onesiphorus,** a faithful presence. Paul writes about him with unusual warmth, describing the one who "showed up, searched me out, and was not ashamed of my chains." (2 Timothy

1:16–17, NIV) This is the friend who doesn't flinch at your failures, doesn't disappear in your valleys, and doesn't pull away when the season gets complicated. They stay.

Name at least one person for each role and tell them. **"Walk with the wise and become wise." (Proverbs 13:20, NIV)**

When the community has hurt you

Hurt is real. Some wounds aren't misunderstandings; they're betrayals. But the answer to being hurt in a community is not avoiding community; it's a *better* community with clearer boundaries. That begins by naming the harm honestly and seeking proper repair; Jesus gives us a path for that in Matthew 18:15-17. It means pursuing wise, safe people choosing character over charisma and fruit over flash, just as Galatians 5 reminds us. It means letting time be a friend, because trust returns in steps, not leaps. And it means staying within the ordinary means of grace: Word, prayer, sacrament, service. God heals in ordinary ways through ordinary saints. Withdrawing to avoid pain often preserves the wound that most needs care. God sets the lonely in families for a reason. (Psalm 68:6, NIV)

Practicing "submit → resist → replace" together

We've used this pattern for temptation; now use it against isolation.

- **Submit:** *Lord, I belong to Your Body; place me where I'm needed and known.* **(James 4:7, NIV)**
- **Resist:** *No* to the lie that I'm better off alone; *no* to the shame that says stay silent.
- **Replace:** Text the ally, show up at group, take a seat in worship, sign up to serve. **Replacing silence with shared life is how isolation loses oxygen.**

Case windows (composites from pastoral life)

Before we talk about strategies or steps, it helps to see what this looks like in real life. These brief snapshots, composites from years of pastoral conversations, show how isolation sneaks in and how grace slowly, stubbornly pulls people back to the center.

The invisible leader. He served everywhere and shared nowhere. A late-night relapse broke the facade. Recovery began not with a platform confession but with a **Barnabas circle**, weekly James 5:16 honesty, and one year of small, stubborn steps. He says now, "I didn't need a spotlight; I needed shoulders."

The wounded volunteer. A sharp comment in a meeting led to quiet resentment and then to quitting. She avoided church for a month, then agreed to coffee. Together we practiced Matthew 18, heard each other, forgave, and reteamed her **with different guardrails**. The wound didn't vanish; it healed.

The overwhelmed mom. Isolation wasn't rebellion; it was exhaustion. Two friends rotated meal drop-offs, one took the toddler to park hour, and a mentor called every Thursday. She says, "I didn't get my life back in a day; I got my people back, and my life followed."

Family practices that fight isolation at home

A home fights isolation through simple, consistent habits. Start with **Word before the world,** even reading one paragraph of Scripture aloud at breakfast, forms a bond and anchors the day in truth. As Deuteronomy reminds us, God's words are meant to be talked about "when you sit… walk… lie down… get up" (Deuteronomy 6:6–7, NIV). Keep a **weekly table**, inviting one person or family and asking the simple question, "Where did you see God this week?" Practice **confessing and forgiving quickly**, modeling apologies that use real words rather than excuses (Colossians 3:13). And **serve side by side**, because nothing braids hearts together like shared mission (Hebrews 10:24). Homes become havens when habits make room for people.

Field Drill (this week)

Awareness turns into strength when it becomes action. These simple steps will help you move from conviction to practice, rebuilding connection one small choice at a time.

- **Name your edge.** Where are you drifting, worship, group, honesty, serve? Write it down and show it to one person.
- **Send the text.** "Could we talk this week? I need to get back in the circle." Put two five-minute calls on the calendar.
- **Pick one gathering and one table.** Commit to a weekly gathering (group or team) and one table (host or accept a meal).
- **Practice one "oneanother."** Choose **to encourage** (1 Thessalonians 5:11), **carry** (Galatians 6:2), or **restore** (Galatians 6:1) and do it for someone by Friday.
- **Pray the family prayer.** *Lord, set the lonely in families, start with ours.* **(Psalm 68:6, NIV)**

REFLECTION & APPLICATION

- Which isolation impulse do you feel most, exhaustion, shame, offense, pride, or busyness, and what swap will you make this week?

- Who are your Barnabas, Nathan, and Onesiphorus? If you don't have them yet, what's your first step to find them?

- What two steps from the 14-day plan will you do first, and who will know?

- Where could you be the one who "holds up arms" this week (Exodus 17:12–13), and what will you practically do?

Out on the savannah, the lion does not waste energy charging a healthy herd; it waits for the one who lingers at the edges. Spiritually, the tactic is the same. But **you are not alone**, and you were never meant to be. The same Lord who warns you about the prowling has given you a people, and the same grace that saves you seats you in a family. So, step back from the edge, take the hands offered, and walk in the middle, alert, anchored, and together. **"By this everyone will know that you are my disciples, if you love one another." (John 13:35, NIV)**

"
WALK WITH THE WISE AND BECOME WISE, FOR A COMPANION OF FOOLS SUFFERS HARM.
"

CHAPTER 8

FINDING STRONG ALLIES

The chainsaws started just after sunrise. A storm had ripped through Sarasota the night before, and a massive oak lay across a neighbor's driveway like a felled giant. I walked over with gloves and a handsaw, useful, I thought, until I saw the size of the trunk. Then other neighbors arrived: one with a saw I'd only seen in hardwarestore displays, another with fuel, another with wedges and know-how. We worked in rhythm, cut, wedge, lift, drag, until the driveway cleared and the street looked like a street again. I kept thinking, *I could never have done this alone.* The job wasn't just big; it demanded a team, each person covering what the others lacked. That morning preached a simple truth: **in a world with real storms, strength is communal, not solo.**

Scripture frames that truth without apology. **"Two are better than one... If either of them falls down, one can help the other up... A cord of three strands is not quickly broken." (Ecclesiastes 4:9–12, NIV)** You're not less spiritual because you need people; you're more biblical. The proverbs add the angle of influence: **"Walk with the wise and become wise, for a companion of fools suffers harm." (Proverbs 13:20, NIV)** Who you walk with shapes who you become. And because the prowling enemy hunts the isolated, allies are not a luxury in the Christian life; they're part of your armor.

Here's the big idea we'll live by: Strong disciples make a deliberate choice to be known on purpose so they can be strong on

purpose, and they pursue relationships that supply what the battle demands: encouragement, correction, prayer, and presence.

Why God writes "we" into your fight

The New Testament's "one another" commands don't decorate Christian life; they power it. **"Encourage one another and build each other up." (1 Thessalonians 5:11, NIV) "Carry each other's burdens, and in this way you will fulfill the law of Christ." (Galatians 6:2, NIV) "Let us consider how we may spur one another on toward love and good deeds... not giving up meeting together... but encouraging one another." (Hebrews 10:24–25, NIV)** These aren't optional extras; they are survival skills in a world with teeth.

Even Jesus embodied this. He ministered to multitudes but walked closely with the Twelve, and in His most vulnerable moments, He drew Peter, James, and John nearer still (Gethsemane). If the sinless Son welcomed companionship in the crush, **we are foolish to attempt faithfulness in isolation.**

What a strong ally is, and isn't

Allies are not fans who flatter you or police who control you. They are wise, courageous, discreet, Scripture-saturated people who help you keep company with Jesus when life pulls you elsewhere. Look for **character over charisma**, because consistency matters far more than charm. Proverbs reminds us, "The way of fools seems right to them, but the wise listen to advice." (Proverbs 12:15, NIV) Choose people with **courage wrapped in kindness**, the kind of friend whose "wounds... can be trusted" because they speak hard truth tenderly (Proverbs 27:6, NIV). Look for those with **Scripture in their mouth and grace in their tone**, the kind of believers who let "the message of Christ dwell among [them] richly... teaching and admonishing one another" (Colossians 3:16, NIV). And seek out people with **discretion**, the ones who hold your story with honor rather than using it as fuel for someone else's. These are the kinds of allies who strengthen your walk instead of distracting it.

Avoid red flags: habitual gossip, an unteachable spirit, disdain for the local church, or fascination with your struggles without commitment to your growth. **Allies are not spectators of your pain; they are participants in your healing.**

Three ally roles you actually need

We previewed these dynamics earlier; here we name them clearly and show how they work together. First, you need an **Encourager**, a Barnabas type, someone who sees grace in you when you can't. Barnabas "saw the evidence of the grace of God and was glad" and strengthened early believers with steady courage (Acts 11). Encouragers today play the same role: they replenish courage without diluting truth. Real encouragement isn't hype; it's hope applied.

You also need a **Truth Teller**, a Nathan type, the friend who stands before you with clarity and covenant. Nathan loved David enough to confront his self-deception, and Scripture says we grow when we "speak the truth in love" (Ephesians 4:15, NIV). Truth tellers aren't harsh; they're holy and helpful, protecting you from the lies you tell yourself.

And finally, you need a **Refreshing Friend**, an Onesiphorus type. Paul wrote of him, "[He] often refreshed me and was not ashamed of my chains... he searched hard for me." (2 Timothy 1:16–17, NIV) This is the friend who shows up when others scatter, steady, practical, unembarrassed by your weakness. Sometimes the most prophetic ministry is simply being present. Together, these three roles form the backbone of strong, biblical allyship.

If you can name one person in each category, you've begun a formidable shield wall.

A few years ago, during a season when ministry felt heavier than usual, I found myself withdrawing without realizing it. I wasn't angry or burned out; I was just tired. My prayers were shorter, my patience thinner, and my confidence quieter. One morning, a friend sent a simple text: "Coffee today?" I almost said no, but something in me knew I needed to say yes.

We sat down, and before I could give a polished "I'm good," he asked, "Where's your heart today really?" The question caught me off guard. I shrugged, tried to laugh it off, but he didn't move on. He waited. And when I finally started talking, the truth spilled out faster than I expected: the weight I'd been carrying, the discouragement I didn't want to name, the decisions that had felt lonely. He listened, then gently said, "You're not meant to carry this by yourself, you know."

It wasn't a dramatic moment, no big revelation, no tears on the table, but it was a **turning point**. His encouragement steadied me, his honesty corrected me, and his presence reminded me that pastors need allies too. Driving home that day, I realized something that reshaped the way I lead: **I wasn't weak for needing people, I was weaker because I had stopped letting them in.** That coffee wasn't just a conversation; it was a rescue.

The gold standard: Jonathan and David

These three roles work together beautifully, and we see their power in one of Scripture's clearest pictures of godly friendship, Jonathan and David.

When fear and danger hemmed David in, Jonathan did something we all need: **"Saul's son Jonathan went to David... and helped him find strength in God." (1 Samuel 23:16–17, NIV)** He didn't merely pep talk him; he **reanchored** him in God's promises. Real allies don't just make you feel better; they **help you stand better.**

And when a brother or sister stumbles? The pattern is gentle restoration, not gossip or grandstanding: **"If someone is caught in a sin, you who live by the Spirit should restore that person gently... Carry each other's burdens." (Galatians 6:1–2, NIV) Restoration is what love does when truth hurts.**

How to find strong allies (a path you can actually walk)

Knowing what an ally is matters, but now you need a path to begin finding them. Scripture and experience give us a surprisingly practical starting point.

Pray specifically. God loves to answer prayers for wise companions. Ask Him to highlight people with character, courage, and capacity.

Plant your life where allies grow. Show up consistently in a small group or serve team; **devote** yourself to shared rhythms, **"They devoted themselves to the apostles' teaching and to fellowship, to the breaking of bread and to prayer." (Acts 2:42, NIV)** Constancy grows connection.

Pursue cross-generational ties. Find someone a few steps ahead and a few steps behind. You need both a **mentor** and a **protégé**; each strengthens you in different ways.

Look for proximity and pattern. Allies are people you can actually see and schedule. Start with those who already display small faithfulness, on time, prepared, and honest.

Scripts for the ask (because clarity helps courage)

The short text (first step):

"Hey, could we grab coffee? I'm building a small circle of two or three people for honest check-ins and prayer. I respect your walk with Jesus and would value your voice."

The table conversation (three moves):

1. Purpose: "I want to stay alert and grow; I don't want to fight alone."

2. Permission: "Will you ask me anything and tell me what I might not want to hear?"

3. Plan: "Could we do a 20minute call each week for a month, and then revisit?"

The confidentiality covenant (one minute):

"What we share stays here unless someone is in danger or asks for help. We choose candor over comfort and grace over gossip."

Why this matters: Permission turns accountability from policing into pastoring.

Rhythms that make allyship real (and sustainable)

Strong allyship isn't built on good intentions alone. It grows through simple, repeatable rhythms that keep relationships honest, connected, and spiritually anchored. Here are two that work in real life.

The 3–3–3 CheckIn

- **Three questions:** Where are you tempted? Where are you grateful? Where are you obeying?
- **Three minutes each:** Keep it focused; don't monologue.
- **Three practices:** Pray *briefly*, assign one next step, send one verse to carry.

The 2–20–2 Rhythm

- **2 minutes daily:** a quick text, "Praying X over you" (2 Tim 1:7; Psalm 27:1; 1 Cor 10:13).
- **20 minutes weekly:** voice call or walk.
- **2 hours monthly:** a longer table for deeper stories, confession, and planning.

The "Ground is tilting" signal

Agree on a phrase that means "Call me now." When temptation spikes, texting that phrase **replaces secrecy with speed. "Confess your sins to each other and pray for each other so that you may be healed." (James 5:16, NIV)**

Guardrails for healthy allyship

- **Keep Scripture central.** Opinion can drift; the Word anchors. Use verses, not vibes.

- **Restore gently.** Aim to heal, not humiliate. **(Galatians 6:1, NIV)**
- **Honor limits.** You're not your friend's Savior or therapist. Encourage professional help when needed; stay a faithful presence.
- **Reject triangulation.** Talk to people, not about them.
- **Stay localchurch rooted.** Strong allies are under shepherds, not above them.

Case windows: three moments when allies changed the outcome

These aren't theories, they're real stories. Here are a few composite moments where strong allies changed the outcome.

The nightshift nurse. After months of quiet exhaustion, she began self-medicating stress. An older woman at church sensed the slide and gently asked questions, then sat with her for an hour after the service. They set a plan: weekly calls, Scripture on the nightstand, and a counseling referral. Today she says, "I didn't find a program; I found a person who stayed." **That friend was a Onesiphorus, refreshing and unashamed.**

The young leader in a comparison spiral. Metrics became a mirror. Two peers formed a triad: one verse to memorize weekly (John 3:27), one service act outside their roles, one social media fast each month. Joy returned as they **replaced** envy with gratitude and mission.

The couple on the brink. A sharp comment in a meeting turned into weeks of cold distance. Another couple invited them to their table, listened without a scoreboard, and guided them through Matthew 18 and Colossians 3. Reconciliation wasn't dramatic; it was **daily**. Presence made peace possible.

Tests for real-time discernment (so allies help you hear Jesus)

When a friend offers counsel, ask: Does this **draw** me toward Christ with conviction and a clear next step, or does it **drive** me away with shame and vague despair? Jesus says, **"My sheep listen to my voice; I know them, and they follow me." (John 10:27, NIV) The Shepherd's voice draws; the enemy's voice drives.** Allies help you tell the difference.

Practicing "submit → resist → replace"… together

You've used this personally; now employ it corporately.

- **Submit (together):** "Jesus, we belong to You; Your Word defines reality." **(James 4:7, NIV)**
- **Resist (together):** Name the specific lie or lure and reject it in prayer and practice.
- **Replace (together):** Fill the gap with Scripture, service, or a call. **If the group doesn't replace the pattern, the pattern will replace the group.**

Family application: allies at home

Strong households normalize team faith. Read a paragraph of Scripture at breakfast. Ask at dinner, "Where did you see God at work today?" Practice fast confession and quick forgiveness. Invite another family to your table twice a month. **"These commandments… Impress them on your children… when you sit… walk… lie down… get up." (Deuteronomy 6:6–7, NIV)** Homes become havens when habits make room for people.

Field Drill (this week)

To help you take a real step this week, here's a simple ally-building field drill.

- **Pray and list five.** Ask God for names of five potential allies (older/peer/younger). Circle two to invite this week.
- **Send the ask.** Use the script above; set a **30day pilot** with a weekly 20minute call. Put it on the calendar before you leave the table.

- **Agree on a checkin plan.** Choose the **3–3–3** or **2–20–2** rhythm and the "ground is tilting" phrase.
- **Write a microcovenant.** Two sentences: confidentiality and candor. Sign it, even if it feels simple.
- **Memorize one ally verse together.** Try **"As iron sharpens iron, so one person sharpens another." (Proverbs 27:17, NIV)** Say it before each call.

REFLECTION & APPLICATION

- Which role is missing in your life right now, encourager, truthteller, or refreshing friend, and who could fill it?

- What keeps you from asking for help, fear of burdening others, pride, or lack of clarity, and what sentence will you use to start the conversation this week?

- When have you been a **Jonathan** or **Onesiphorus** for someone else? What would it look like to do that again, on purpose?

- Which rhythm (3–3–3 or 2–20–2) best suits your season? What day and time will you protect for it?

When we finished clearing that oak, no one bragged about their chainsaw. We looked at a clean street, shared a laugh, and checked the next house. That's allyship in miniature: **not heroes collecting credit, but friends sharing burdens** until neighborhoods (and souls) become passable again. The enemy still prowls; the storms still form. But when you lock arms with wise, steady people under the authority of Jesus, **you will find that faith stands taller and fear runs shorter**, because God delights to make His strength visible through a people who refuse to fight alone. **"By this everyone will know that you are my disciples, if you love one another." (John 13:35, NIV)**

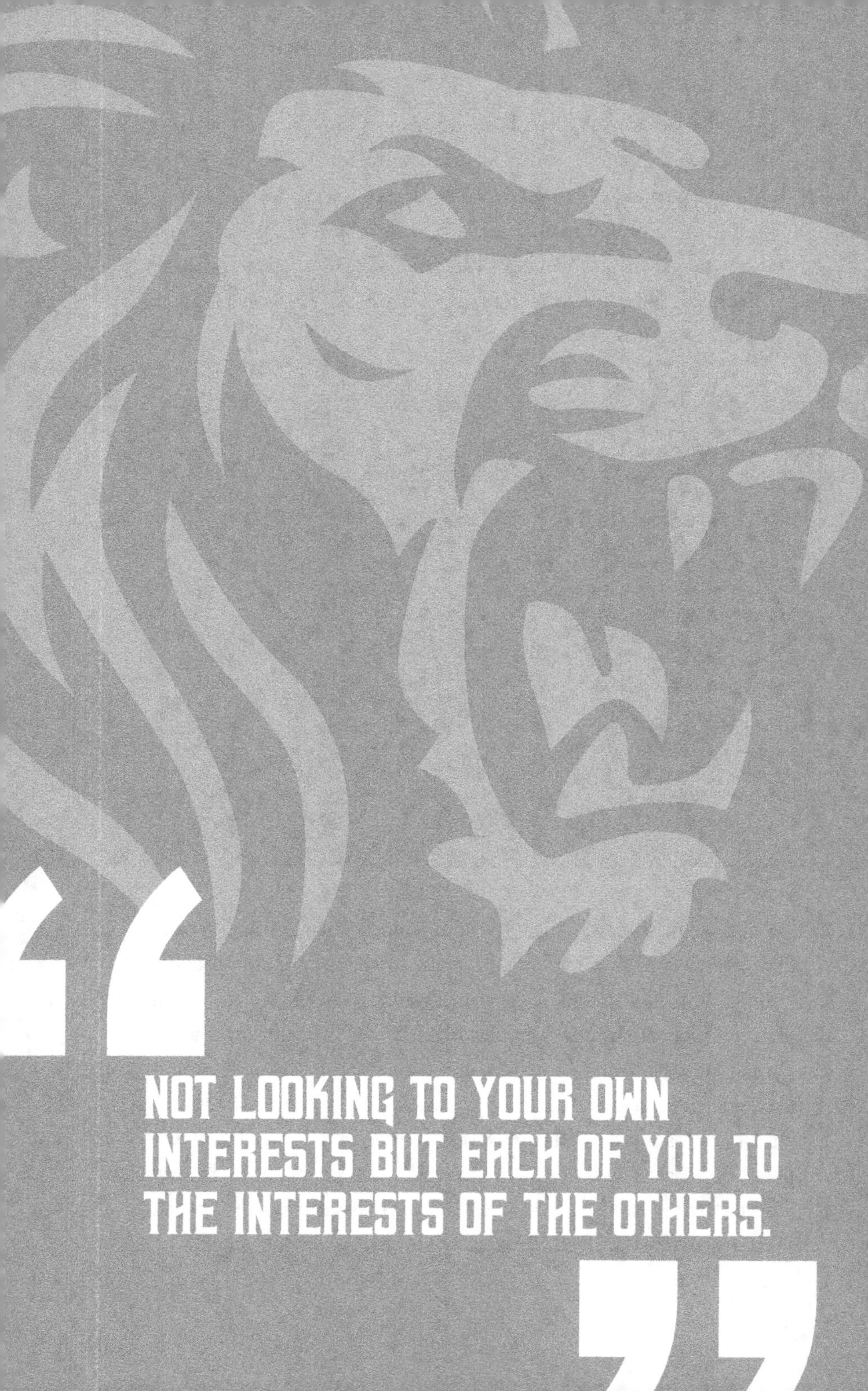

"
NOT LOOKING TO YOUR OWN INTERESTS BUT EACH OF YOU TO THE INTERESTS OF THE OTHERS.
"

CHAPTER 9

WATCHING OUT FOR OTHERS

It started with a shoulder shrug and a halfsmile. After group, one of our guys moved a little faster than usual toward the parking lot. He'd been quieter for weeks, cracking jokes to deflect any real conversation. "I'm good," he said, tightening his grip on the truck door. But when I asked, "Are you really?" he paused. Eyes glassed over. A long breath. Then the story tumbled out, exhaustion, a secret slide, a fight at home he regretted. We prayed right there between tailgates. Two others from group drifted over, no fanfare, just presence. One put a hand on his shoulder and said, "We've got you." What could have turned into isolation became an intersection, because somebody noticed and somebody stayed.

That's the pulse of this chapter: in a world with a prowling enemy, **mature disciples don't only stand firm for themselves, they watch the perimeter for one another, and they step in with grace and courage when love is needed.** We're not spiritual tourists; we're a rescue team.

Why watching out is part of discipleship (not an optional extra)

When the New Testament describes church life, it refuses solitary faith. Paul calls us to a reflex of othermindedness: **"Not looking to your own interests but each of you to the interests of the others."** (Philippians 2:4, NIV) That is not busybody meddling; it is Christshaped love that pays attention. It sounds like Hebrews' cadence, where we're told to **"consider how we may spur one another on toward love and good deeds"** and **"not [to] give up meeting together... but [to] encourage one another."** (Hebrews 10:24–25, NIV)

Peter adds a global, bracing reason to stay near one another: **"Resist him, standing firm in the faith, because you know that the family of believers throughout the world is undergoing the same kind of sufferings."** (1 Peter 5:9, NIV) If a lion hunts stragglers, it is pastoral wisdom, not paranoia, to keep the flock close.

Embedded truth to hold onto: Love looks up, looks out, and steps toward. It scans the row on Sunday, the text thread on Tuesday, the table on Thursday, and chooses presence over passivity.

What we're watching for (common warning lights)

We are not sin spotters; we are shepherd-hearted friends. Still, love pays attention. It notices patterns before pain turns into fallout, because early warning lights usually blink long before someone breaks. Sometimes the signal is **sudden distance,** a reliable friend goes quiet, starts missing gatherings, cancels at the last minute, or replies more slowly than usual (Hebrews 10:24–25). Other times it shows up as **increasing secrecy** conversations grow vague, humor replaces honesty, and simple check-ins feel strangely evasive (Proverbs 28:13).

A third light is a **brittle spirit** small slights begin to loom large, cynicism hardens, and gratitude thins out (Hebrews 12:15). Or it may be **unshared pressure**, when new stress loss, conflict, workload, or disappointment is met with isolation instead of invitation (1 Thessalonians 5:14). And sometimes the warning is **compromise creep,** those "just this once" choices that repeat until convictions are quietly relabeled as "personal freedom" (Romans 13:14).

When those lights begin to blink, love moves first not with a lecture, but with a steady presence that says, "You're not a project; you're my brother... my sister."

Paul sets our tone: **"If someone is caught in a sin, you who live by the Spirit should restore that person gently... Carry each other's burdens, and in this way you will fulfill the law of Christ."** (Galatians 6:1–2, NIV) Notice three anchors:

Restoration always begins with the right posture. We move toward repair, not toward ruining someone's reputation; the goal is to restore, not to expose. And we do it **gently, not grandly**, letting our tone reflect the kindness of Christ rather than the weight of our own frustration. True restoration also means we **carry, not crush,** we shoulder the weight someone can't bear in the moment instead of adding new burdens to an already heavy heart.

Jude adds nuance for differing situations: **"Be merciful to those who doubt; save others by snatching them from the fire; to others show mercy, mixed with fear..."** (Jude 22–23, NIV) Some souls need space and patience; others need bold interventions; all need mercy.

A simple Restoration Pathway (four moves you can remember)

Restoring someone rarely happens by accident. It requires a posture of grace and a plan that keeps you steady when emotions run high. Here's a simple pathway you can carry into any hard moment. Think **P.A.C.E.,** because love that helps others endure keeps a steady pace.

P – Pray & prepare. Before a word to them, speak many words to God. Ask for humility, clarity, and timing. Remember Jesus' pattern: **"First take the plank out of your own eye."** (Matthew 7:5, NIV)

A – Approach gently & ask real questions. Lead with honor: "I could be wrong, but I'm concerned about you. Can I check in?" Then listen, **really** listen, without filling the silence. **"Everyone should be quick to listen, slow to speak and slow to become angry."** (James 1:19, NIV)

C – Clarify truth & craft a next step. Speak **truth in love** (Ephesians 4:15, NIV). Name what's good, what's harmful, and what's next, one concrete, doable step within a week (a call, a confession, a boundary, an appointment).

E – Engage for the long haul. Don't drop a hard word and disappear. Text midweek. Meet again. **"Encourage one another daily… so that none of you may be hardened by sin's deceitfulness."** (Hebrews 3:13, NIV)

In all four: keep grace near the surface. **"There is now no condemnation for those who are in Christ Jesus."** (Romans 8:1, NIV) That promise is oxygen for repentance.

How to speak hard truth without doing harm

Speaking the hard truth begins with examining your own aim. Before you say anything, ask whether your goal is their good before God or simply your own relief. If it's the latter, wisdom says to wait and pray. When the time is right, **choose a setting that is carefully** private, not performative, just as Jesus instructs in Matthew 18:15. And when you speak, use *"I"* language and Scripture: "I'm concerned because I love you, and this word from the Lord's heart gives me conviction…" Let the Word carry the weight, not your frustration.

As you talk, **name grace as clearly as you name guilt**. Point to the way back, confession, repair, guardrails, community, so the path forward feels possible, not crushing. And don't disappear after the hard conversation; **agree on follow-up**, because love that stays is what turns a moment into a ministry. Truth without love wounds, and love without truth withers. The cross gives us both a holy verdict and an open welcome.

Carrying burdens vs. enabling patterns (wise limits)

Romans gives us a purposeful paradox: "We who are strong ought to bear with the failings of the weak" (Romans 15:1, NIV), yet Paul also says, "each one should carry their own load" (Galatians 6:5, NIV). Loving well means knowing the difference. In moments of crisis, we **bear what they cannot,** bringing meals, offering prayer, and showing up with presence and practical help. But in seasons of growth, we **refuse what they must carry themselves,** excuses, secrecy, and unkept commitments. Sometimes loving someone means **inviting wider help**, whether from pastors, counselors, or recovery groups, because love is never a lone-ranger project. And through it all, we **honor safety**; if someone is in danger, self-harm, abuse, or violence, we act immediately, involve the right authorities, and bring pastors into the loop. Shepherds protect, and love moves wisely.

Bible windows that shape our imagination

Scripture paints vivid windows that shape our imagination for what watching out for one another really looks like. In Exodus, when **Moses' arms sagged**, Israel sagged with him; but when **Aaron and Hur held his arms up**, the people prevailed. That moment isn't just history it's a template for community: hold up the tired one until strength returns (Exodus 17:12–13, NIV). Then there's **Jonathan and David**, where Jonathan "went to David... and helped him find strength in God." He didn't flatter David; he re-anchored him in the promises of God (1 Samuel 23:16–17, NIV). And the picture continues in the early church, where "they devoted themselves... to fellowship... to prayer." (Acts 2:42, NIV) Restoration didn't thrive on occasional dips into community but on stubborn, consistent rhythms of shared life. These scenes invite us into a way of living where strengthening one another is normal, not exceptional.

A gentle discerner: which voice am I echoing?

In every hard conversation, ask, *Am I echoing the Shepherd or the Accuser?* **"My sheep listen to my voice... and they follow me."** (John 10:27, NIV) The Shepherd's voice **draws** with conviction and a clear next step; the Accuser's voice **drives** with shame and vague doom. If your words can't be prayed and obeyed, revise them until they can.

"Watching out" in everyday practice (microrhythms you can start this week)

Here are a few small, everyday practices that turn the heart of this chapter into real movement, simple rhythms that make "watching out" normal, not dramatic.

- **The three-question text:** *Where are you tempted? Where are you tired? Where are you thankful?* Rotate that text among two or three friends each week.
- **The 10-minute parkinglot rule:** If someone lingers after worship with that far-off stare, initiate, don't assume. "Can I walk with you to your car?"
- **The CPR checkin for groups: C**elebrate (one grace), **P**ressure (one burden), **R**equest (one specific prayer). Keep it moving; keep it honest.
- **The "ground is tilting" phrase:** Agree on a phrase that means "call me now." Use it. Respond fast. (James 5:16, NIV)

When someone stumbles (a map for restoration)

At some point, someone you care about will fall. The question isn't *if* it will happen, but *how* you'll respond. Scripture gives us a roadmap for that moment.

1. Name the fall with clarity and compassion. Euphemisms fog repentance; harshness freezes it.

2. Bring the sin into the light with God and a person. "Confess your sins... pray... be healed." (James 5:16, NIV)

3. Repair what's repairable. Apologize, repay, rebuild trust through kept commitments.

4. Rebuild supports. Counselor referral, recovery meetings, device boundaries, new routes for lonely hours.

5. Reengage mission. Serving reorients the self away from self. **"Let us... spur one another on toward love and good deeds."** (Hebrews 10:24, NIV)

Remember Jude's spectrum: mercy for the doubter; urgency for the endangered; reverent caution for tangled situations (Jude 22–23, NIV). Tailor your approach to the person in front of you.

Case windows (composites from pastoral life)

Sometimes it helps to see how these principles unfold in actual lives. These brief case windows drawn from years of pastoral conversations show how grace steps in when someone is close to slipping.

"I'm fine." A young professional kept repeating the words as eye contact faded. Two friends instituted the CPR check-in for eight weeks, showed up with dinner twice, and joined him at a first counseling session. He says now, "The problem didn't evaporate, but the shame did. And that changed everything."

The quiet relapse. A leader whiteknuckled through latenight temptation until he lost his grip. Instead of staging a tribunal, two elders met him with **Galatians 6:1** gentleness, wrote a 30day plan (filter, curfew, nightly psalm, weekly counselor), and rotated check-ins. Consequences were real; condemnation wasn't. Repentance grew roots.

The tired caregiver. A mom caring for an aging parent missed church for weeks. A couple from her row started tagteaming Sunday pickups and Wednesday meals. They didn't fix the situation; they lowered the waterline. She returned to worship with tears and relief.

Building a "restoration culture" in your church or group

Building a **restoration culture** in a church or group begins with leaders who are willing to go first. When pastors and group leaders share something real they're repenting of or learning, it creates safety for everyone else. Vulnerability at the top releases honesty in the room.

It also means teaching Matthew 18 as a pathway of *peacemaking*, not punishment: moving from private conversation, to bringing a witness, to involving leaders only when necessary, each step aimed at gain, not gotcha (Matthew 18:15–17, NIV). A restoration culture removes unnecessary barriers by creating clear pathways, cards, or QR codes for counseling referrals, recovery ministries, and benevolence help, so no one has to wonder where to turn when they're struggling.

It also celebrates quiet wins with joy rather than gossip: "A brother came back to the group after a hard season, praise God," and nothing more. And it gives people simple, gospel-shaped language to open doors: "I'm here. You're not crazy. Let's ask Jesus what to do next." A community that practices these rhythms becomes a place where restoration isn't rare; it's normal.

Family application: watching out at home (without turning home into a police station)

At home, watching out for one another happens through simple, steady practices. Start by **setting a daily question** at the table: "Where did you see God at work today?" Keep it ordinary and short; consistency beats intensity (Deuteronomy 6:6 7, NIV). Then **practice quick confession and fast forgiveness**, because you cannot export what you do not practice (Colossians 3:13, NIV). Teach your family a gentle version of **"see something, say something,"** where siblings learn to voice concern without shaming or policing. And finally, **rotate intercession,** let one person pray by name for another family member before bed. Watching out begins in prayer, and these small rhythms quietly shape a home into a place of grace and spiritual safety.

Prayers you can pray when words are hard

- **For the wandering:** *Shepherd, find and carry them. Give me gentleness and courage.* (Luke 15)

- **For the weary:** *Lord, strengthen feeble knees and lift weak hands; let Your joy be their strength.* (Hebrews 12:12; Nehemiah 8:10)
- **For the hard conversation:** *Set a guard over my mouth; let kindness and truth walk together.* (Psalm 141:3; Ephesians 4:15)
- **For the restoring community:** *Make us a people who carry burdens without carrying gossip.* (Galatians 6:2)

Field Drill (this week)

- **Scan & step.** On Sunday (or your next gathering), ask God to highlight **one** person. Send a sameday text: "Thinking of you, anything I can pray for?"
- **Pick a partner.** Choose one ally and agree on a **twoweek CPR checkin** (Celebrate, Pressure, Request) by text every other day.
- **Write a 90second plan** for a tough conversation you've avoided (one honor sentence, one concern, one clear next step). Put it on your calendar within seven days.
- **Resource list.** Save a note with your church's counselor referrals, recovery ministries, and benevolence process so help is one tap away.
- **Pray Hebrews 3:13** over two people daily: "Lord, use me to encourage them today so sin's deceit won't harden their hearts."

- Who around you is giving off "warninglight" signals, distance, secrecy, brittleness, and what gentle first step will you take?

- Which part of the **P.A.C.E.** pathway do you tend to skip (prepare, approach, clarify, engage), and how will you practice it this week?

- Where do you need to set a **loving limit** so you're carrying a burden without enabling a pattern?

- When have others "held up your arms," and how can you honor that by doing the same for someone else?

On the hill above the battlefield, Moses' arms sagged as the sun dropped. The people faltered, until Aaron and Hur took their places, one on each side, **holding him steady until the victory came**. (Exodus 17:12–13, NIV) That is a picture for every small group, every marriage, every church row: **when one grows tired, the others lift; when one is tempted, the others walk close; when one drifts, the others call them home.** The enemy still prowls, but love that watches and moves leaves him hungry. **"By this everyone will know that you are my disciples, if you love one another."** (John 13:35, NIV)

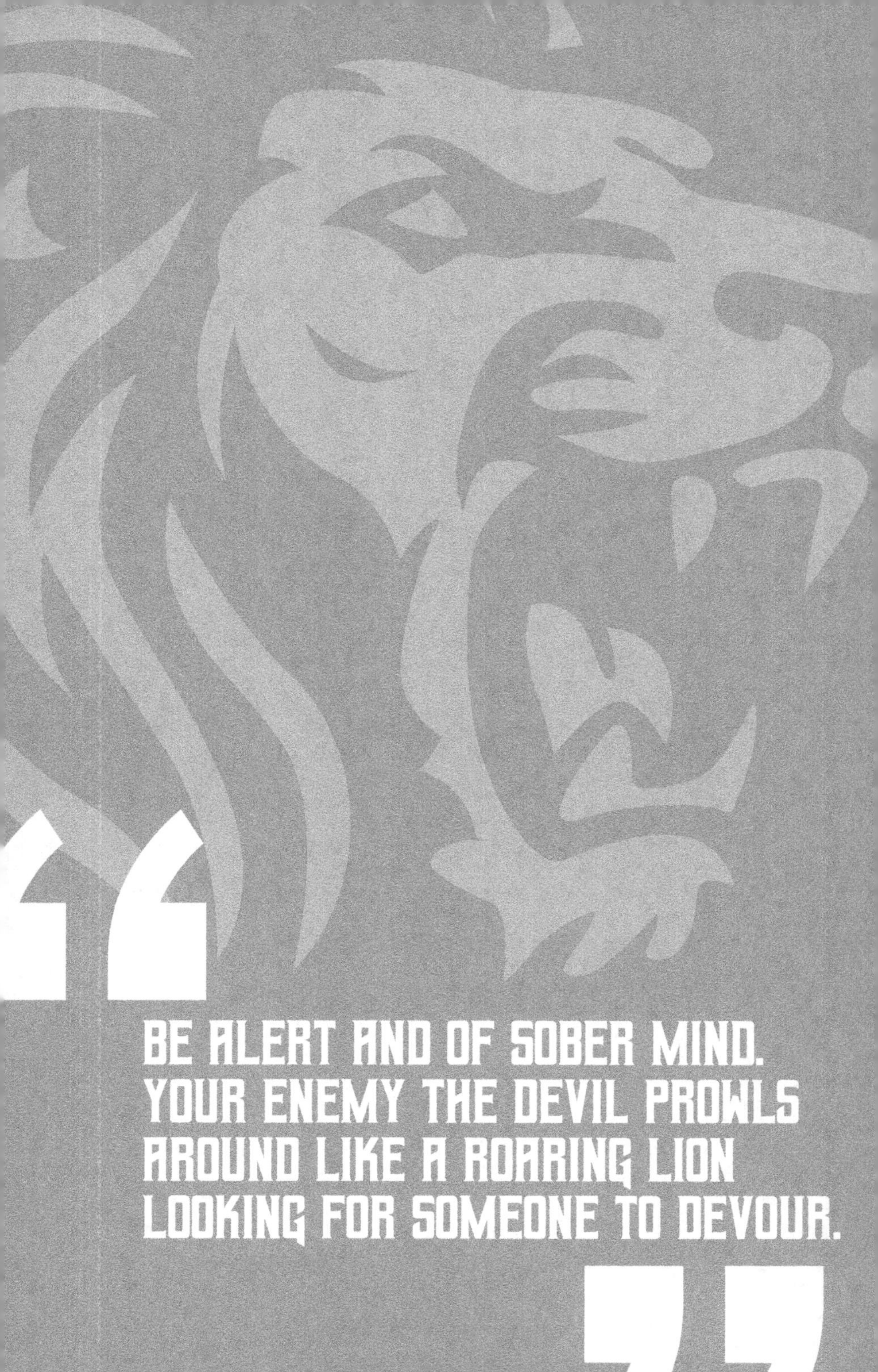

BE ALERT AND OF SOBER MIND.
YOUR ENEMY THE DEVIL PROWLS
AROUND LIKE A ROARING LION
LOOKING FOR SOMEONE TO DEVOUR.

CHAPTER 10

GUARDING THE NEXT GENERATION

The red flags were snapping hard in the Gulf breeze. Lifeguards had already pulled two swimmers out of a rip current that morning, and their whistles cut through the surf every few minutes. Our kids were tugging at us, "Can we go in now?", and we wanted to say yes. But first we walked to the waterline and watched. We pointed to the flags, traced the sideways drift of foam that betrayed the rip, and found the space between the two watchtowers. Then we made a plan: *only between the flags, eyes on the lifeguard's chair, out if the whistle blows, and we swim together.* We didn't give a fear speech; we gave a strategy. In dangerous water, **love doesn't say "be brave," love teaches how to be safe**. And that is the heart of this chapter. Real threats don't call for panic or passivity; they call for clear, practiced, gospelshaped preparation, for us and for our kids.

Parents and pastors, mentors and grandparents, teachers and coaches, we all feel the rip currents in this cultural moment. Messages about identity, truth, and purpose roar louder than the surf. That is why Peter's wake-up call belongs on our refrigerators as much as our pulpits: **"Be alert and of sober mind. Your enemy the devil prowls around like a roaring lion looking for someone to devour."** (1 Peter 5:8, NIV) If a predator hunts the vulnerable, then guarding the next generation isn't a side project; it is frontline discipleship.

What God asks of us (and why it matters now)

Scripture places first responsibility for faith formation not on programs but on people, especially parents. Moses speaks to ordinary households, not experts: **"These commandments that I give you today are to be on your hearts. Impress them on your children. Talk about them when you sit at home and when you walk along the road, when you lie down and when you get up."** (Deuteronomy 6:6–7, NIV) That is a vision of everyday, everywhere discipleship.

Paul says the same to families in Ephesus: **"Fathers, do not exasperate your children; instead, bring them up in the training and instruction of the Lord."** (Ephesians 6:4, NIV) And the psalmist widens the call beyond the nuclear family to the whole people of God: **"We will tell the next generation the praiseworthy deeds of the Lord... so the next generation would know them... and they would put their trust in God."** (Psalm 78:4, 6–7, NIV)

In a culture that often catechizes our kids faster than we do, the church can support and equip, but it **cannot** replace the home. That's why we keep repeating a line I want woven into your habits: **we don't force faith; we form hearts**, patiently, consistently, in the ordinary flow of days. Formation is not coercion; it's care.

Three ditches to avoid

Parents and mentors tend to drift into one of three unhelpful modes. **Fear-based control** clamps down so tightly that rules replace relationship, and kids learn to perform rather than trust Jesus. On the opposite side is **free-range abdication**, where in an effort to avoid "forced religion," we outsource formation or let kids "decide when they're ready." That's not freedom, it's neglect. Hope isn't a strategy, especially when a hunter is on the prowl. And then there's **performance Christianity**, where we celebrate outcomes, grades, goals, good behavior, and church attendance without ever speaking to the heart. Kids become accomplished...and exhausted.

Celebrating excellence is good; confusing excellence with identity is not. We delight in their gifts, but we anchor their worth in the grace of Jesus.

Gospel-shaped formation refuses all three extremes. It is truthful without being harsh and tender without being hollow. It keeps grace and guidance in the same sentence, and that is what helps the next generation grow in both strength and trust.

A couple of years ago, a dad in our church asked if we could grab coffee. His son had shifted almost overnight, quieter at home, more anxious, grades slipping, hiding behind headphones. "I don't know what happened," he said, "and I feel like I'm already behind." He assumed something dramatic had occurred, but when we traced it back, it wasn't one big event, it was a slow drift. A new friend group, more late-night scrolling, fewer meals together, and a dozen silent questions about identity he didn't know how to ask.

The dad told me, "I realized I've been reacting to storms instead of preparing for them." So he made three small changes that week. **Word before world** at breakfast, even if it was just one paragraph. **Screen Sabbath** on Saturdays, half a day with phones in a basket and people in the room. **One weekly mission moment:** bringing a meal to a neighbor, writing a thank-you note, or picking up trash on their walk. None of it felt dramatic.

Three weeks later, he pulled me aside, eyes wet. "He's talking again," he said. "He's asking questions again. It's like the fog is thinning." Nothing had magically fixed itself, but small, consistent habits began to steady the home and give his son something solid to grab onto. His words stuck with me: **"I thought I needed a big breakthrough. Turns out, I just needed to start building a rhythm."**

Know the waters your kids are swimming in

The enemy's oldest plays now wear new uniforms. He still lies (John 8:44), but more often he "masquerades as an angel of light" (2 Corinthians 11:14, NIV). Many destructive ideas arrive dressed as compassion, authenticity, or self-care. So we teach our kids to name the currents and check the flags. Sometimes that current is **deception**, when a message contradicts God's Word but calls itself loving.

In those moments, we help them test it: "Do not conform to the pattern of this world, but be transformed by the renewing of your mind." (Romans 12:2, NIV) Other times the current is **distraction**, because the endless scroll is never neutral. Attention shapes affection, which is why Paul urges us to fill our minds with whatever is true, noble, right, and pure (Philippians 4:8, NIV). And often the current is **despair**, as anxiety and comparison speak loudly into young hearts. When that happens, we walk them back to the Shepherd: "The Lord is my light and my salvation, whom shall I fear?" (Psalm 27:1, NIV)

As we name these cultural currents, we do it without demonizing our neighbors. Our children are not trained to fight people; they're trained to follow Jesus faithfully in people-filled places.

The biblical order: submit → resist → replace

Kids learn what we *practice*, not only what we *preach*. So when pressure hits, we model James' sequence: **"Submit yourselves, then, to God. Resist the devil, and he will flee from you."** (James 4:7, NIV) We yield to Jesus' authority **first**, say no to lies **next**, and then **replace** the space with something holy, a verse spoken, a call to a mentor, an act of service. This is one of the clearest family mantras you can give: *submit, resist, replace*. And yes, say it **with them**, not just to them.

A family rule of life (simple, durable practices)

This is not about building a bunker but about building reflexes. Remember the watchman language from Nehemiah, **"We prayed to our God and posted a guard day and night."** (Nehemiah 4:9, NIV) Prayer doesn't replace preparation; it powers it. Let that shape your trellis:

Daily

- **Word before world.** Even one paragraph aloud at breakfast. Ask, "What does this show us about God?" Then pray one sentence each. (Deuteronomy 6:7; Psalm 143:8, NIV)
- **Gratitude at the table.** Everyone shares one gift from the day. Gratitude shrinks shadows.
- **Evening blessing.** A hand on a shoulder and a short prayer: "May the Lord make you strong and kind in Jesus." (Numbers 6:24–26, NIV)

Weekly

- **Worship together.** Not as consumers but contributors. Sit together, serve together. **"Not giving up meeting together... but encouraging one another."** (Hebrews 10:25, NIV)
- **Screen Sabbath (halfday).** Phones in the basket; people in the room. Talk, walk, play, nap, unhurried presence.
- **One mission moment.** A simple shared act of mercy, write a note, take a meal, pick up litter, because mission braids hearts.

Monthly

- **Story night.** Tell a family faith story ("When God provided..."). Psalm 78 says we **"will tell the next generation the praiseworthy deeds of the Lord."** (Psalm 78:4, NIV)
- **Practice the hard convo.** Take one relevant topic, identity, sexuality, friendship, screens, and discuss with Scripture and compassion. The enemy thrives in silence; truth thrives at the table.

As you build these rhythms, remember the line we set in the Introduction: **what you normalize in peacetime determines how you respond in battle.** These small habits are your family's peacetime drills.

A "Philippians 4:8" media plan (curate, don't just block)

Filters and fences matter; catechesis matters more. Teach kids to ask, "What is this content training me to love?" Then give them tools:

- **Common spaces for screens** and **common charged** devices overnight.
- **Cowatch and talk**: "What was beautiful? What was broken? What would Jesus say to this character?"
- **Replace, don't only remove**: when you limit one feed, add rich inputs, Scripture apps, biographies, worship, nature, art. **"Whatever is excellent or praiseworthy, think about such things."** (Philippians 4:8, NIV)

Agewise conversations (not one talk, but many)

- **Childhood (6–10):** God made you on purpose (Genesis 1–2); Jesus loves you and listens; the Bible is true and good. Memorize short verses; practice short prayers. **"How can a young person stay on the path of purity? By living according to your word."** (Psalm 119:9, NIV)
- **Middle school (11–13):** Identity, friendship, feelings, screens. Teach "draws vs. drives": the Shepherd's voice **draws** with grace and a next step; the enemy's voice **drives** with shame and doom. (John 10:27, NIV)
- **High school (14–18):** Calling, wisdom, sex, money, work, justice, leadership. Anchor them in 2 Timothy 3:14–17, **"the Holy Scriptures... are able to make you wise for salvation... All Scripture is Godbreathed and is useful..."** (NIV)

Each stage: short, frequent, scriptedbyScripture, delivered with warmth. Kids remember a thousand threeminute talks more than one threehour lecture.

Boundaries are not legalism; they're love

When Jesus speaks starkly about cutting off what causes us to stumble (Matthew 5:29–30), He commends **seriousness**, not selfharm. Love adds guardrails because futures are at stake. Write **if/then** predecisions *together*:

- **If** it's after 10 p.m., **then** devices sleep in the kitchen.
- **If** a friend sends a sketchy link, **then** I text Dad/Mom a screenshot and we talk.
- **If** I feel a comparison spiral, **then** I log off for 24 hours and write three thankyou prayers.

"The prudent see danger and take refuge." (Proverbs 27:12, NIV) Teach kids that wise boundaries protect freedom; they don't choke it.

Church and home: allies, not substitutes

The local church is your training partner. Youth ministry is not a holding tank; it's a greenhouse. Partner well:

- **Know your leaders** and invite their voice. Ask what they're teaching; echo it at home.
- **Invite crossgenerational mentors**: a college student who loves Jesus can be a heroic "older sibling" for your middleschooler.
- **Serve together**: kids who sweat for the church tend to love the church.

Remember the sober line from earlier in the book: **if we don't disciple our kids, the culture will**, and the culture is tireless. So let your home and church become a joyful, unhurried resistance to that tide.

Case windows (composites from pastoral life)

Sometimes the best way to understand how these principles play out is to see them in real stories. Here are a few composite snapshots from pastoral life that show what it looks like to guard the next generation with wisdom and grace.

The quiet middleschool drift. Grades good, attitude fine, but the Bible gathered dust and the phone grew roots. The parents didn't panic; they pivoted. "Word before world" at breakfast (one paragraph, one question, one sentence prayer), Wednesday night youth became nonnegotiable again, and they added a Saturday "screen Sabbath." Within a month, the currents felt different; laughter and questions returned.

The highschool senior with loud questions. He loved Jesus but felt tugofwar over sexuality and identity conversations at school. His parents didn't preach a monologue; they opened a Bible, kept a pace of compassion, and kept inviting mentors to the table. Together they memorized **"Do not conform… but be transformed by the renewing of your mind."** (Romans 12:2, NIV) He didn't get a script; he got a spine and a shepherd.

The blended family battling schedules. Weekon, weekoff made rhythms hard. Their plan: Sunday worship regardless of which house, Wednesday FaceTime to read a psalm, and a onceamonth "service Saturday." Small, stubborn habits outlasted complicated logistics.

When you feel late to the party

Maybe the kids are teenagers and you're just now waking up. Don't be paralyzed by "if only." God specializes in late starts and new mercies. Start small and honest:

- **Confess** to your kids where you've coasted; ask forgiveness for mixed messages. (Colossians 3:13, NIV)
- **Name** one rhythm you'll begin this week (Word before world; table gratitude; Wednesday youth).
- **Invite** a mentor to your table; humility opens doors your lectures never will.
- **Pray** out loud for your kids by name. Nothing steadies a home like parents who pray.

When a hard question comes, slow down and use three moves:

1. **Honor** the question: "Thank you for trusting me with that."

2. **Open** the Word: "Let's see what Jesus says."

3. **Offer** a next step: a verse to carry, a boundary to keep, a person to include.

You won't always have perfect answers; you can always give faithful presence. **Love that stays is often the loudest apologetic.**

Field Drill (this week)

- **Write a onepage family plan.** Four headings: Word, Worship, Table, Tech. One small practice under each. Tape it inside a cabinet door. (Deuteronomy 6:6–7, NIV)

- **Set two if/then predecisions.** Let your kids help write them; let your teens own them. (Proverbs 27:12, NIV)

- **Adopt "submit → resist → replace."** Practice it with a real temptation moment this week. (James 4:7, NIV)

- **Schedule one crossgenerational connection.** Invite a trusted older student/mentor for pizza and prayer. (Hebrews 10:24–25, NIV)

- **Screen Sabbath.** Choose a halfday this weekend. Put the phones in a basket; put people in the room. Share highs/lows and end with a simple blessing (Numbers 6:24–26, NIV).

When the flags snap and the whistles sound, you don't shame your kids for wanting to swim; you stand with them between the flags, eyes on the guard, and you make a plan. Spiritually, do the same. Walk your children between the flags of the Word and the people of God, eyes on Jesus, the Lion of Judah. He loves them more than you do. And as you build habits of watchful love, remember the promise that buoys every parent's heart: **"The one who is in you is greater than the one who is in the world."** (1 John 4:4, NIV) So step steady, teach gently, and trust boldly, because **real threats demand real adjustments**, and grace gives you everything you need to make them.

PART IV
STAND FIRM IN HOPE

"
CAST ALL YOUR ANXIETY ON HIM
BECAUSE HE CARES FOR YOU.
"

CASTING YOUR CARES, NOT CARRYING THEM

We were loading sandbags before a storm, the kind of Florida morning where the air already feels like a wet blanket. A few of us formed a line, passing bags hand to hand into the truck. Then I tried to hurry the process, grabbed two at once, and felt my back bark. Our neighbor laughed kindly and said, "Preacher, the goal isn't to prove you're strong; it's to move the weight." He was right. When you're bracing for wind, wisdom isn't heroics, it's transfer. And that is the spiritual move Peter invites: not an act of bravado, but a transfer of weight from you to the One who cares. **"Cast all your anxiety on him because he cares for you."** (1 Peter 5:7, NIV) In a book about soberminded vigilance and a prowling enemy, that sentence is not a soft aside; it's strategy. **In the life of faith, you don't win by carrying more, you stand by casting more.**

Peter's charge sits inside a paragraph that sets our posture for the whole battle: **"Humble yourselves, therefore, under God's mighty hand, that he may lift you up in due time."** Then: **"Cast all your anxiety on him because he cares for you."** And then the line we've been living by: **"Be alert and of sober mind… resist him, standing firm in the faith."** (1 Peter 5:6–9, NIV) The order matters. We **submit** (humble under His hand), we **cast** (transfer the weight), and then we **resist** (with a lightened heart and clear head). **Stand** under God before you stand against evil, and in between, lay your burdens down.

What "cast" actually means

Peter's verb is vivid. To "cast" (*rhiptō*) is to **throw** something off you onto another. It's fisherman language, not therapist language. He's not telling you to admire your anxieties; he's telling you to hurl them where they belong, onto a willing, strong Savior. When you do, you're not being careless; you're honoring the CareGiver. **Casting isn't poetic; it's practiced.** It sounds like, "Jesus, here is the situation, the person, the deadline, the fear. I'm handing it to You, again, because **You** care."

Jesus had already said the same thing in an even more tender key: **"Come to me, all you who are weary and burdened, and I will give you rest... For my yoke is easy and my burden is light."** (Matthew 11:28–30, NIV) He does not invite you to perform; He invites you to **transfer**.

Why do we keep carrying what we're supposed to cast

If casting is so simple, why do our shoulders still ache? Often, it's because **pride** whispers, *I've got this.* We wouldn't say it out loud, but we function like an atheist's strategy without surrender, effort without prayer. Scripture corrects us gently: "Trust in the Lord with all your heart and lean not on your own understanding." (Proverbs 3:5, NIV) Pride prays last; humility prays first. Other times, the obstacle is **control**, the belief that *I can't let this go.* We confuse stewardship with sovereignty, and casting feels like losing our grip. But God loosens white knuckles with His promise: "Do not fear, for I am with you... I will strengthen you and help you." (Isaiah 41:10, NIV)

Sometimes the barrier is **habit** anxiety has become familiar, even identity-shaping. But familiar isn't the same as faithful. The psalmist models a better pattern: "Cast your cares on the Lord, and he will sustain you." (Psalm 55:22, NIV) And then there is **shame**, the voice that says, *I should be stronger by now.* We assume that bringing God the same burden again proves to be a failure. It does, and that is exactly where grace comes rushing in: "My grace is sufficient for you, for my power is made perfect in weakness." (2 Corinthians 12:9, NIV)

Anxiety is a weight to cast, not a cross to carry. The cross has already been shouldered, and it wasn't yours.

Casting and the lion: why this belongs in a warfare book

There's a reason Peter puts the casting command right beside the warfare warning; it's not random placement; it's strategic.

Peter ties casting to resisting because **a heavy heart is easier to hunt.** When cares pile up, temptations feel stronger, lies sound truer, and our reactions get rash. The enemy loves a hurried, harried mind. That's why Paul links a non-anxious posture to clear prayer and guarded peace: **"Do not be anxious about anything, but in every situation, by prayer and petition, with thanksgiving, present your requests to God."** What follows? **"And the peace of God, which transcends all understanding, will guard your hearts and your minds in Christ Jesus."** (Philippians 4:6–7, NIV) Casting is not retreat; it's **how your inner guard takes its post.**

And notice the word Peter chooses for God's posture: **care.** Not grudging tolerance. Not distant oversight. **Care.** The universe's Sovereign regards your Monday list with a Father's attention. **We don't cast into a void; we cast into care.**

What we cast vs. what we carry

Scripture holds two truths in tension: **"Carry each other's burdens"** (Galatians 6:2, NIV) and **"each one should carry their own load"** (Galatians 6:5, NIV). How do we hold both? Think **boulder** vs. **backpack.** A "load" is the ordinary weight of responsibility: repent, reconcile, show up, do the next faithful thing. A "burden" is the crushing weight you cannot shoulder, guilt that lingers after you've confessed, outcomes you can't control, tomorrow's weather in your soul. The first, you carry **with** God and **with** others; the second, you cast **onto** God, and you invite others to help with the lift.

A few months ago, I met with a man from our church who looked worn down in a way I hadn't seen before. He said, "I'm not doing anything wrong, I'm just tired in my bones." He wasn't talking about sin; he was talking about strain. Work had piled up, his dad's health was declining, and every night he found himself lying awake, replaying the same "what if" scenarios until sunrise.

I asked him what he did with those thoughts, and he smiled sadly: "Honestly? I just carry them. I don't want to bother God with something I should be able to handle." Then he said the sentence that revealed everything: "I feel guilty asking for help when I'm the one who's supposed to be strong."

We opened 1 Peter 5:7 together, slowly, like thirsty people reading a fountain sign: "Cast all your anxiety on him because he cares for you." He stared at the verse for a long moment and said, "I've been praying like God is disappointed in me, not like He cares for me." That week, he started using a simple casting sentence every morning: *Jesus, I hand You this because You care.* A few days later, he texted me, "The problems are still here, but they're not all on me anymore."

Nothing magical happened, but the weight moved. And sometimes, that's the miracle.

A map for the moment the weight rises

When you feel the surge, tight chest, racing mind, clenched jaw, move through this four-step drill. (I keep it scribbled on an index card.)

1. **Name it.** "This is anxiety about ______." (Clarity breaks the fog.)

2. Kneel to it. "Father, **I submit** to You." (James 4:7, NIV)

3. Cast it. "Jesus, **I throw this** onto You because **You care**." (1 Peter 5:7, NIV)

4. Replace it. Speak Scripture and take one embodied step: breathe slow, go for a five-minute gratitude walk, or text an ally. **If you don't replace, you'll replay.**

Add Paul's filter for the mind's playlist: **"Whatever is true, whatever is noble, whatever is right, whatever is pure... think about such things."** (Philippians 4:8, NIV) **Casting empties; replacing fills.** That's how peace stays.

Jesus and the anxious disciples: watch & pray, rest & walk

In the garden, Jesus gave His exhausted friends a simple, brilliant rhythm: **"Watch and pray so that you will not fall into temptation. The spirit is willing, but the flesh is weak."** (Matthew 26:41, NIV) Watching is attention; praying is dependence. That same Lord later stood by a sea and said, **"Come to me, all you who are weary and burdened."** (Matthew 11:28, NIV) The sequence is consistent: **look up, come close, hand it over, walk on.**

Obstacles that sound holy (but aren't)

Some obstacles to casting sound holy at first, but they aren't. One of them is **stoicism**, the inner vow that says, *"It's fine. I'll power through."* That isn't strength; it's strain. God doesn't ask you to white-knuckle your way forward. He invites honest requests: "Let us then approach God's throne of grace with confidence... to find grace to help us in our time of need." (Hebrews 4:16, NIV) Another obstacle is **pious delay**, the instinct to fix everything you can before you pray. It's the reverse order. Pray first so you're doing is aligned, not anxious, because "in all your ways submit to him, and he will make your paths straight." (Proverbs 3:6, NIV) And then there is **selective casting**, the quiet belief that says, *"I trust God with eternity, not Tuesday."* But

God wants your calendar as much as your creed; "in everything… present your requests to God." (Philippians 4:6, NIV)

Sustained surrender beats occasional panic. Make casting hourly if you need to. It's a habit, not a ritual.

Case windows (composites from pastoral life)

Sometimes the best way to understand casting is to see how it plays out in real lives. These brief pastoral composites show what it looks like when ordinary people transfer their cares to a God who carries them.

The anxious parent. The "whatifs" multiplied at 2 a.m. Instead of doomscrolling, she made a **care transfer** ritual: write the worry on a card, pray it aloud (**1 Peter 5:7**), place the card in a box on the nightstand labeled "His." Each morning, she read one card back to God and left it there. The circumstances didn't change overnight. **Control loosened. Peace grew.**

The pressured leader. Decisions stacked up; sleep thinned out. He scheduled three fiveminute "watch & pray" bells (10:30, 2:30, 8:30). Each bell: breathe, **cast**, speak **Philippians 4:6–7**, send one honoring text. The team noticed: fewer sharp edges, more steady presence.

The student with racing thoughts. Before exams she looped: *If I don't ace this…* Her mentor taught the fourstep drill, added **Psalm 23** as a walking prayer, and asked for a nightly "care transfer" text: **casted** items only, no explanations. That discipline turned monologue into dialogue, her heart with God, her life with community.

The care of God (why casting isn't wishful thinking)

Peter anchors the command in God's character: **"because he cares for you."** (1 Peter 5:7, NIV) That's covenant language. He cared enough to send the Son (John 3:16). He cares enough to number your hairs (Luke 12:7). He cares enough to **"be close to the brokenhearted and** save those who are **crushed in spirit."** (Psalm 34:18, NIV) Your anxiety does not repel Him; it **summons** Him. This is why David can talk to his fear this way: **"When I am afraid, I put my trust in you."** (Psalm 56:3, NIV) **Fear isn't failure; it's a doorway to trust.**

And when the weight returns (because it will), you don't apologize for being human; you **practice being a child.** Children with good fathers don't rehearse the mechanics of carrying; they **ask for help. "Your Father knows what you need before you ask him."** (Matthew 6:8, NIV)

Tying it to the book's cadence

We've been repeating a rule all along, **submit → resist → replace.** Casting is the hinge between submission and resistance. You humble under God's hand (submission), **throw** Him the freight (casting), and then stand firm against the schemes (resistance), filling the space with truth, gratitude, and obedience (replacement). Do this in a body, not a bubble: **"Carry each other's burdens."** (Galatians 6:2, NIV) Your friend's text, "Tell me what you're casting today", might be the guard at their gate.

Five practices that make casting a reflex

Casting becomes easier when it becomes a rhythm, not an emergency response. One simple practice is the **"Care Transfer" sentence,** saying out loud, in specific and present-tense language, "Jesus, I hand You this." If you can write it, write it; if all you can manage is a sigh, Romans 8:26 says God knows how to interpret that too. Another habit is the **"two pockets" practice:** keep two small cards with you. In the left pocket, write "My part today" just one obedient next step. In the right pocket, write "God's part" for the things you cannot control. At lunch, check your pockets and swap anything you've grabbed back from Him.

A third rhythm is the **gratitude swap**. Anxiety narrows attention, while gratitude widens it. After you cast a care, name three gifts, even tiny ones. Scripture instructs us, "Give thanks in all circumstances." (1 Thessalonians 5:18, NIV) Fourth, keep **Scripture on your tongue**. Choose three verses: one for fear (Psalm 27:1), one for identity (1 John 3:1), and one for provision (Matthew 6:33-34). Speak one whenever you feel that familiar lift in your chest. And finally, use the **ally text**. Agree on a simple phrase, "Ground is tilting." When you send it, your ally prays Philippians 4:6–7 over you and replies with one truth, not ten tips. These small moves turn casting from a concept into a reflex.

When the burden includes real grief

Casting is not denial; it's dependence. Some anxieties arrive attached to loss you can't fix. Scripture doesn't shame tears; it bottles them (Psalm 56:8). You can cast **and** lament. You can **"pour out your hearts to him, for God is our refuge."** (Psalm 62:8, NIV) Pair lament with hope: **"The Lord is close to the brokenhearted."** (Psalm 34:18, NIV) You're not dropping your grief; you're refusing to carry it **alone**.

When the "after a little while" feels long

Peter promises that **"after you have suffered a little while,"** God will **"restore you and make you strong, firm and steadfast."** (1 Peter 5:10, NIV) "A little while" can feel like forever. Keep a record of small restorations, answers that came, mercies that met you, and strength that surprised you. Remembering fuels repeating. **Cast again, because He cared again.**

- **Morning transfer (2 minutes).** Kneel if you can. Pray 1 Peter 5:6–10 in your own words, humble, **cast**, be alert, resist, hope. Name **one** care and speak the casting sentence: "Jesus, I hand You _______ because You care."

- **Noon pockets check (60 seconds).** Review your two cards. Move anything from *My part* to *God's part* if it belongs there. Do your one obedient step before lunch.

- **Evening examen (5 minutes).** Ask: Where did I carry instead of cast? What did God carry for me? Read **Philippians 4:6–7** aloud. Place one written care into a "His box" (literal or digital). Close it.

- **Ally rhythm.** Pick one person. Exchange a single daily text that starts, "Casting:" and lists one item. Reply only with a verse and "Praying."

- **Sabbath the scroll.** Choose a halfday. No news, no feed. Walk, rest, and pray **Psalm 23** as a slow conversation. Let your Shepherd set the pace.

REFLECTION & APPLICATION

- Which counterfeit strength keeps you carrying, **pride, control, habit, or shame**, and what would repentance look like this week?

- What "boulder" are you trying to shoulder that belongs in God's hands? What "backpack" (your part) will you carry today?

- What three verses will you keep on your tongue to replace anxious loops with truth?

- Who will be your **casting ally** for the next fourteen days, and what phrase will mean "call me now"?

The neighbor with the sandbags was right. The goal isn't to prove you're strong; it's to move the weight. Spiritually, that's not a metaphor; it's a command, backed by a promise. **"Cast all your anxiety on him because he cares for you."** (1 Peter 5:7, NIV) So make the transfer, hourly if you must. Lift your empty hands again under **"the God of all grace,"** and expect Him, **"after you have suffered a little while,"** to **"restore you and make you strong, firm and steadfast."** (1 Peter 5:10, NIV) The lion still prowls, but lighthearted saints, light because they keep casting, are awfully hard to devour.

FOR THE SPIRIT GOD GAVE US DOES NOT MAKE US TIMID, BUT GIVES US POWER, LOVE AND SELFDISCIPLINE.

CHAPTER 12

LIVING IN CONFIDENCE, NOT FEAR

The harness dug into my hips as I shuffled to the edge of the platform. Twentyfive feet below, a field of scrub and palmetto fanned out like a carpet of green. Our guide clipped my rope into the belay line, tugged twice, and smiled: "You don't conquer the height; you trust the rope. When you step, the rope holds." I nodded, then stared into the space between "knowing" and "stepping." Finally, I leaned forward, felt the sudden drop, and catch!, the line went taut. My body learned in a second what my mind already knew: **confidence isn't the absence of risk; it's the presence of trust**. From that moment on, I moved differently across the course, not because the height changed, but because my weight was somewhere stronger than me.

That's the move Scripture invites when fear tries to rule. Peter's realism about the "roaring lion" (1 Peter 5:8) lives in the same paragraph as a steadying promise: **"Cast all your anxiety on him because he cares for you."** (1 Peter 5:7, NIV) Fear is real; care is nearer. The Holy Spirit reframes our posture: **"For the Spirit God gave us does not make us timid, but gives us power, love and selfdiscipline."** (2 Timothy 1:7, NIV) In other words, **the gospel doesn't make you louder; it makes you steadier**, power for obedience, love for people, and a sound mind for the moment. When the enemy roars to paralyze, we answer with practiced trust that keeps moving.

What fear does, and why it's a discipleship issue

Fear is not merely a feeling you have to "get over"; it's often part of the enemy's strategy to keep you from faithful presence. Jesus named the thief's intent clearly: "The thief comes only to steal and kill and destroy; I have come that they may have life and have it to the full." (John 10:10, NIV) Fear shrinks your life to the size of your worries, while faith expands it to the size of God's care. It works subtly.

Fear distracts your purpose, you begin second-guessing God's call, stalling in obedience, turning inward. God answers with His steady promise: "So do not fear, for I am with you... I will strengthen you and help you." (Isaiah 41:10, NIV) **Fear distorts your vision** like Israel facing giants; your problems start to loom larger than God's promises. "We seemed like grasshoppers in our own eyes" (Numbers 13:33, NIV) is the confession of a people who forgot their Deliverer. **Fear isolates** shame, and "what ifs" push you from people, even though courage often comes back when shoulders are close (Ecclesiastes 4:12, NIV). And **fear gives a foothold** anxiety becomes an inner narrator, and Paul warns us plainly: "Do not give the devil a foothold." (Ephesians 4:27, NIV) Fear doesn't just unsettle you; it opens a doorway for lies to sound logical.

None of this means we pretend threats aren't real. Biblical courage isn't bravado; it's obedience under pressure. That's why God's refrain to every trembling heart is relational before it's tactical: "Do not be afraid... for the Lord your God will be with you wherever you go." (Joshua 1:9, NIV)

Eyes up in the wind: Peter on the water

Matthew tells it plainly: Peter stepped out of the boat at Jesus' word and walked. But **"when he saw the wind, he was afraid, and, beginning to sink, cried out, 'Lord, save me!'"** Jesus **"immediately reached out his hand and caught him."** (Matthew 14:30–31, NIV)

Notice the rhythm: a command, a step, a surge of fear, a cry, a catching hand, a gentle correction. **Christian confidence isn't swagger; it's a Savior's grip.** It's learning, often in motion, to keep your eyes where your weight already is, on Jesus.

Confidence defined (and defused from counterfeits)

Let's say it clearly: **Christian confidence is not selfassurance; it's Saviorassurance.** It's not a big personality; it's a big God. It's not denial of danger; it's **defiant trust** in the Presence that walks into danger with you. **"The Lord is my light and my salvation, whom shall I fear?"** (Psalm 27:1, NIV) When fear argues that you're alone, the gospel answers: **"Never will I leave you; never will I forsake you."** (Hebrews 13:5, NIV) When fear insists that this will finish you, grace replies: **"My grace is sufficient for you, for my power is made perfect in weakness."** (2 Corinthians 12:9, NIV)

Four gospel shifts from fear to confidence

1. Identity: from orphaned to adopted.

Fear thrives on scarcity: *It's all on me; I'm not enough.* The gospel answers with sonship: **"See what great love the Father has lavished on us, that we should be called children of God!"** (1 John 3:1, NIV) **Confidence grows where you remember whose you are.**

2. Attention: from storm to Savior.

Peter sank "when he saw the wind." Attention is formation. So set your mind: **"Whatever is true... noble... right... pure... think about such things."** (Philippians 4:8, NIV) **What wins your attention will shape your emotion.**

3. Pace: from frantic to faithful.

Hurry is fear's accelerator. God's gift is a sane cadence: **"In repentance and rest is your salvation, in quietness and trust is your strength."** (Isaiah 30:15, NIV) **Sabbath is not laziness; it's confidence that God runs the world.**

4. Company: from alone to together.

Confidence is contagious. **"Encourage one another and build each other up."** (1 Thessalonians 5:11, NIV) Shields lock best when shoulders are close (Ephesians 6). **You don't need to feel fearless when your friends feel faithful.**

Pray it through: from panic to guarded peace

Paul doesn't shame anxious hearts; he hands them a practice: **"Do not be anxious about anything, but in every situation, by prayer and petition, with thanksgiving, present your requests to God."** What happens next? **"The peace of God... will guard your hearts and your minds in Christ Jesus."** (Philippians 4:6–7, NIV) That verb *guard* is military. **Peace becomes your posted sentry**, not because circumstances are simple, but because **presence is near**. Try this in the moment:

- **Name:** "Father, I'm afraid about _______."
- **Kneel (submit):** "I place this under Your hand." (James 4:7, NIV)
- **Cast:** "Jesus, I throw this onto You because **You** care." (1 Peter 5:7, NIV)
- **Replace:** Speak one verse; take one embodied step (a slow breath, a short walk, a quick call). **If you don't replace, you'll replay.**

When fear feels reasonable (wisdom vs. worry)

Scripture never equates vigilance with anxiety. Nehemiah's crew **"prayed to our God and posted a guard day and night."** (Nehemiah 4:9, NIV) That's confidence with plans. **Preparation isn't panic; it's love in advance.** So, lock the doors, set the boundary, write the if/then, **and** refuse the inner swirl that pretends omniscience. God carries what you can't (Galatians 6:2/6:5 tension). You carry today's obedience; He carries tomorrow's outcomes.

When fear is tied to real loss

Some of our fear rides on grief we didn't choose. Scripture doesn't rebuke tears; it bottles them (Psalm 56:8). You can **cast** and **lament**: **"Pour out your hearts to him, for God is our refuge."** (Psalm 62:8, NIV) Walk with wise counselors and trusted friends; medicine and therapy can be gifts of common grace. None of that competes with prayer; it often gives your prayers traction.

Three practices that train confidence

One simple way to retrain your heart toward confidence is to practice the **three-line breath prayer** three times a day. As you inhale, pray, *"Jesus, You are with me."* As you exhale, pray, *"I cast this care."* Then speak one anchoring truth aloud: *"The one who is in you is greater than the one who is in the world."* (1 John 4:4, NIV) This small rhythm slows your body and recenters your attention on Presence, not pressure.

Another practice is **one-step obedience**. When fear says, *"You can't,"* shrink the moment to the next faithful move, send the email, make the apology, take the walk. Courage grows by inches, not leaps, and God meets us in motion, not in paralysis.

A third training tool is shaping **faith headlines** short, memorized truths that answer your three loudest fears. For provision fear, hold onto Jesus' promise: *"Seek first his kingdom... and all these things will be given to you."* (Matthew 6:33, NIV) For safety fear, speak David's confession: *"The Lord is my light and my salvation, whom shall I fear?"* (Psalm 27:1, NIV) And for fear about the future, remember Jesus' closing words: *"Surely I am with you always, to the very end of the age."* (Matthew 28:20, NIV) These headlines become the truths you reach for when fear starts writing the story.

Case windows (composites from pastoral life)

Sometimes the clearest way to see what confidence looks like in real life is to watch how it unfolds in ordinary people. These brief snapshots show what happens when fear meets practiced trust.

The waiting room. She refreshed the patient portal like it was a liturgy. Together we wrote a "care transfer" card: one column for "my part today," one for "God's part today." Each refresh, she whispered **Philippians 4:6–7** and texted one gratitude to a friend. The results came with both relief and new steps. Fear didn't vanish; **it lost the steering wheel.**

The small business owner. Cash flow dipped; sleep followed. He set three alarms (10:30/2:30/8:30) for a 90-second castandreplace. He also called two mentors. Within weeks, the numbers weren't fixed, but his presence with his team was. **Confidence looked like clear eyes and honest plans.**

The student and the stage. She loved worship but dreaded the mic. A friend met her twenty minutes early to pray **Joshua 1:9** and to practice slow breaths. "Eyes up, heart open, sing to the One who's here." The voice didn't become bolder than the fear; **the trust became louder than both.**

Practicing "submit → resist → replace" against fear

We've used this sequence throughout the book, and here's the fear-specific version because fear is often the scheme behind other schemes (Ephesians 6:11). When fear rises, **submit** first: "Jesus, I place this moment under Your authority" (James 4:7, NIV). Then **resist**: "In Your name, I refuse the lie that I am alone, helpless, or doomed" (1 Peter 5:9, NIV). And finally, **replace;** put Scripture on your tongue, gratitude in your mouth, and love in motion toward a neighbor. According to John, "perfect love drives out fear" (1 John 4:18, NIV), so replacing fear's voice with acts of love becomes courage in motion.

At home, we don't minimize threats or magnify them; **we model trust**. Keep the cadence simple: **Word before world** (one paragraph aloud at breakfast), **table gratitude** ("one good gift" each), **evening blessing** (a hand on a shoulder with **Numbers 6:24–26**). When kids voice fears, honor them, then anchor them: "Thank you for telling me. Let's ask Jesus what He says," and read **Psalm 56:3, "When I am afraid, I put my trust in you."** (NIV) **Confidence is caught from calm adults who keep casting.**

Field Drill (this week)

- **Daily 2minute suitup for courage.** Pray 2 Timothy 1:7 in your own words: "Spirit of power, love, and a sound mind, govern me today." Speak one faith headline (Matthew 28:20; Psalm 27:1; Matthew 6:33).
- **Noon "rope check."** Ask: Where is my weight, on my control, or on Christ? If you've grabbed the load back, make a onesentence care transfer: "Jesus, I hand You ______ because You care." (1 Peter 5:7, NIV)
- **Write two if/then scripts** for your fearspike hour. *If* email dings after 9 p.m., *then* phone sleeps in the kitchen and I pray Psalm 23 aloud. *If* conflict looms, *then* I ask for wisdom (James 1:5) and schedule a calm conversation.
- **Ally text.** Choose one person. Exchange a single daily text that begins, "Casting:" with one line only; reply with one verse and "Praying."
- **Sabbath the scroll** for a half day. Take a slow walk and pray **Philippians 4:6–7** with each step.

REFLECTION & APPLICATION

- Which fear most narrows your obedience right now, provision, safety, reputation, the future, and which **faith headline** will you carry to meet it?

- Where do you confuse anxiety with vigilance? What *Nehemiah plan* (pray **and** post a guard) would express **confidence with preparation** this week?

- Whose calm courage helped you stand in a hard season? How will you be that shoulder for someone else before Friday?

- What is one step you'll take today, small but concrete, that says, "My weight is on the rope," not on my control?

You won't always feel brave. You don't have to. The point of the harness wasn't to make me fearless; it was to hold me when I stepped. That's the gospel's gift: **you are held**, even when the wind is loud. So, lift your eyes, steady your breath, and take the next faithful step. Jesus has already said it, and it still holds on Tuesday mornings and hospital Thursdays: **"In this world you will have trouble. But take heart! I have overcome the world."** (John 16:33, NIV) The lion still roars, but the **Lion of Judah** still reigns, and **confidence grows wherever your trust shifts from your grip to His.**

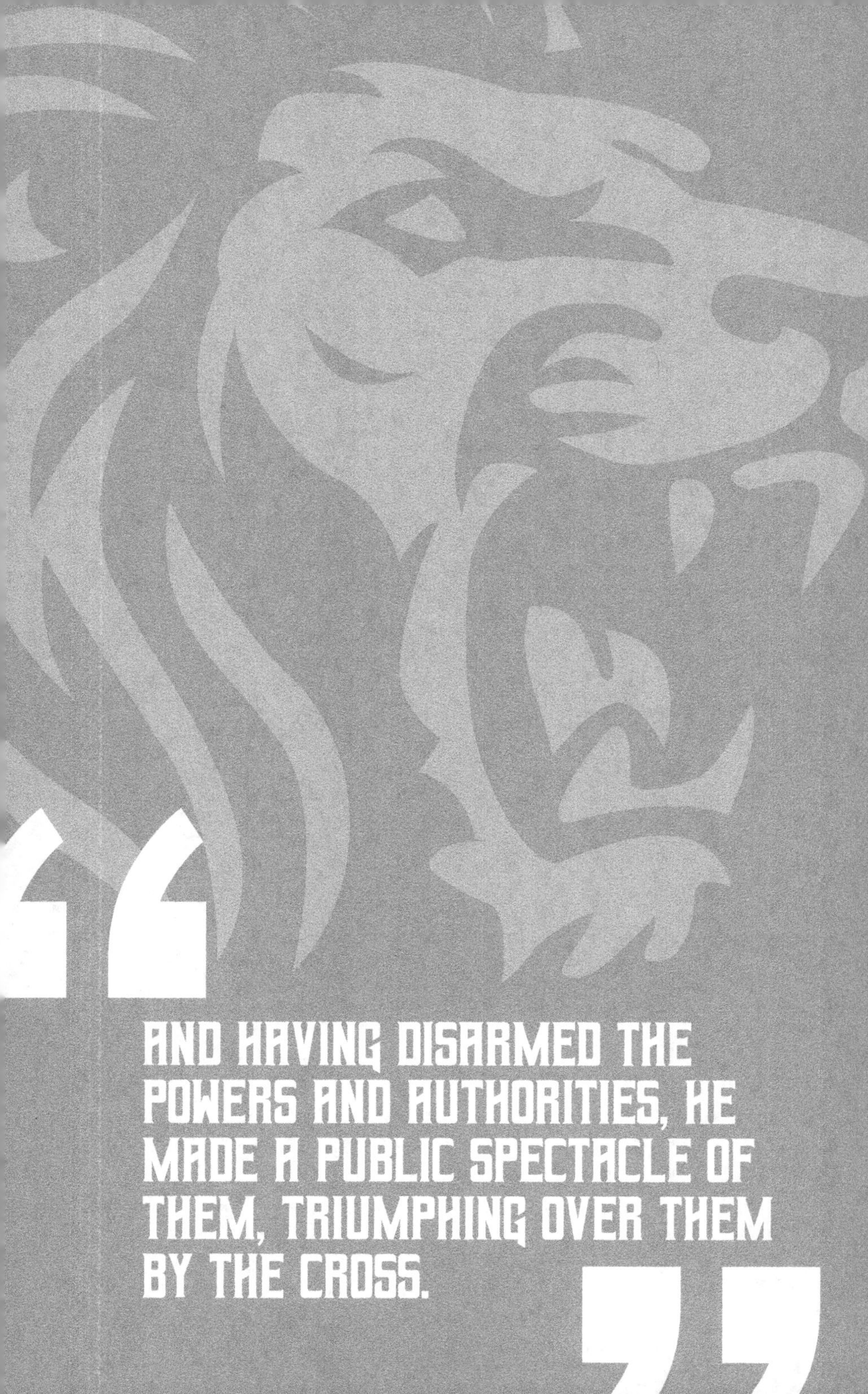
"
AND HAVING DISARMED THE
POWERS AND AUTHORITIES, HE
MADE A PUBLIC SPECTACLE OF
THEM, TRIUMPHING OVER THEM
BY THE CROSS.
"

CHAPTER 13

THE ULTIMATE END OF THE LION

The scoreboard told the truth before anyone wanted to admit it. Fourth quarter, less than a minute left, down by three possessions. The other team still ran plays, but everyone in the stadium knew the outcome. You could feel the shift, desperation in their huddle, confidence in ours. They kept blitzing, taking risky shots, burning timeouts they couldn't afford. **When the result is settled, frantic plays don't change the end; they only reveal who knows the clock is running out.** That's where we live spiritually: the outcome of the war is already decided, and the enemy's late-game fury can't rewrite the final score.

Scripture is unblinking about that final score. John says of the crucified and risen Christ, **"And having disarmed the powers and authorities, he made a public spectacle of them, triumphing over them by the cross."** (Colossians 2:15, NIV) Past tense: disarmed, triumphed. Yet the same Bible fastforwards to the last whistle and shows us the end of our adversary: **"And the devil... was thrown into the lake of burning sulfur... and will be tormented day and night for ever and ever."** (Revelation 20:10, NIV) **The cross secured the victory; the judgment will display it.** We live in the gap between the wins, **the "already" of Christ's triumph and the "not yet" of Satan's final removal,** and that inbetween explains both the roar and our hope.

Two anchors: what's finished and what's future

Call it a two-line confession that steadies your soul:

- **Finished:** At the cross and empty tomb, Jesus decisively broke the tyrant's claim. He "bound the strong man" and plundered his house (cf. Mark 3:27), so much so that Jesus could say, **"Now the prince of this world will be driven out."** (John 12:31, NIV)

- **Future:** At Christ's return, the verdict becomes visible. The deceiver who still prowls will be silenced, judged, and removed (Revelation 20:10, NIV). **The story doesn't end with a stalemate; it ends with a sentence.**

Holding both truths keeps us from two equal errors: panic (as if the outcome were uncertain) and passivity (as if the battle were imaginary).

Why the end matters now

1) Courage without bravado.

You don't need swagger to be steady. **"The one who is in you is greater than the one who is in the world."** (1 John 4:4, NIV) That is not theory; it is oxygen. **We act boldly not because the enemy is small, but because the Savior is supreme.**

2) Endurance without despair.

Paul ties the long obedience to the long victory: **"Stand firm. Let nothing move you. Always give yourselves fully to the work of the Lord... your labor in the Lord is not in vain."** (1 Corinthians 15:58, NIV) **The finish line reframes the fatigue of the race.**

3) Sobriety without cynicism.

Revelation describes a devil who "knows that his time is short" and so is enraged (Revelation 12:12, NIV). That explains the spike in pressure some seasons: **rage is the emotion of a losing adversary on a clock.** We stay alert, not alarmed.

4) Hope without illusion.

Christians are not naïve about darkness; we are stubborn about dawn. **"He must reign until he has put all his enemies under his feet."** (1 Corinthians 15:25, NIV) That includes the enemy you're facing on Tuesday.

What the enemy can, and cannot, do

The Bible grants the enemy **reality** while denying him **sovereignty**. He can **prowl** (1 Peter 5:8), stalking and scheming, but he cannot **prevail** over Christ's church Jesus has already promised, "the gates of Hades will not overcome it." (Matthew 16:18, NIV) He can **accuse** (Revelation 12:10), whispering old failures in fresh tones, but he cannot **condemn** those who are in Christ, for "there is now no condemnation for those who are in Christ Jesus." (Romans 8:1, NIV) He can **tempt** (Matthew 4), offering shortcuts and shadows, but he cannot **force** obedience to sin: "No temptation... has overtaken you except what is common to mankind... [and] God will also provide a way out." (1 Corinthians 10:13, NIV) And though he can **roar**, he cannot **write your future** the promise still stands: "Never will I leave you; never will I forsake you." (Hebrews 13:5, NIV)

Satan is dangerous but not decisive; Jesus is gentle and decisive.

Living in the "already / not yet" without whiplash

Think of a chess endgame where checkmate is guaranteed even though a few moves remain. That's Christian time, **the outcome is sealed; obedience is how we play out the win.** Three adjustments make that posture livable:

A. Fight from the cross, not for it.

When accusation circles, you do not negotiate with your past; you announce your position: **"God made him who had no sin to be sin for us... so that in him we might become the righteousness of**

God." (2 Corinthians 5:21, NIV) **We don't fight for victory; we fight from it, but we still fight.**

B. Practice present resistance with future hope.

James gives the order that keeps you from selfreliant striving: **"Submit yourselves, then, to God. Resist the devil, and he will flee from you."** (James 4:7, NIV) Submit → resist → replace (with truth, prayer, community). **Hope does not cancel effort; it powers it.**

C. Trade doomscrolling for kingdomseeking.

Jesus' counsel is not denial but redirection: **"Seek first his kingdom and his righteousness."** (Matthew 6:33, NIV) Attention is discipleship, what holds your gaze will train your heart.

What the final defeat reveals about God

Justice that isn't hurried, yet never late.

The dragon's end tells you that **God's patience is not God's permission.** Peter says the Lord is patient, "not wanting anyone to perish" (2 Peter 3:9, NIV), yet the day comes. Mercy and justice are not rivals in God; they are harmonized in Christ.

Kingship that covers the cosmos.

Jesus declares, **"All authority in heaven and on earth has been given to me."** (Matthew 28:18, NIV) Evil is not an equal and opposite force; it is rebellion on borrowed time. **Your courage rises as your Christ enlarges.**

Love that refuses to lose you.

Paul heaps words on top of words to make the point: **"In all these things we are more than conquerors through him who loved us."** (Romans 8:37, NIV) The end of the lion is good news because the heart of your King is steadfast.

How the end shapes Tuesday's decisions

Knowing the end of the story doesn't make life easy, but it does make life *clear*. When you remember the verdict that's already been written, it begins to shape the choices you make on ordinary Tuesdays. Here's what that looks like.

Persevere where you're tempted to quit. Suffering never gets the last word; Jesus does. Peter promises that "after you have suffered a little while, [He] will himself restore you and make you strong, firm and steadfast." (1 Peter 5:10, NIV) So keep sowing good seed. Harvest has a schedule, even when your season feels stalled.

Repent where you're tempted to drift. A settled victory is not a license to coast; it's a summons to come home. The Spirit's conviction is always future-oriented. He corrects you because He's keeping you for the day of Christ. Repentance is not doom; it's direction.

Rejoice where you're tempted to brood. Joy is not denial; joy is defiance. Scripture calls us to "rejoice in hope, be patient in affliction, faithful in prayer." (Romans 12:12, NIV rendering) When Paul and Silas sang in a prison cell (Acts 16), it wasn't naïve optimism; it was theological clarity. They knew the clock and the King.

Witness where you're tempted to hide. If Christ will finish what He started, then your neighbor's story is not closed. Pray, speak, serve with confidence. The Lion of Judah still rescues lambs, and He often does it through the steady courage of His people.

Case Windows (where the ending changed the middle)

Here are a few real-life glimpses of what it looks like when the certainty of Christ's final victory begins reshaping the middle of someone's story.

A mom in the long middle of caregiving.

Grief had a daily commute. She started praying Revelation's future into today's fatigue: **"He will wipe every tear from their eyes."** (Revelation 21:4, NIV) The tears didn't stop; the despair did. Her "why" didn't get smaller, but **her "Who" got closer.**

A young believer facing old shame.

Night brought the loudest accusations, *remember that season, that sin?* The answer became a spoken liturgy: **"There is now no** condemnation for those who are in Christ Jesus." (Romans 8:1, NIV) She paired it with a text to an ally and five minutes in a psalm. The accuser still knocked; he no longer set the terms.

A pastor under cultural headwinds.

Each headline felt like another gust. He stopped pacing and started praying the end: **"Now have come the salvation and the power and the kingdom of our God, and the authority of his Messiah."** (Revelation 12:10, NIV) Then he kept preaching Christ with clarity and tenderness. **Hope made his voice gentle and stubborn.**

Common Misreads (and better readings)

Even with a clear ending, we often misinterpret what victory means for life now. Here are a few common misunderstandings and the better readings Scripture offers.

Misread: "If the devil's defeated, resistance is optional."

Better: Defeat fuels resistance. **Christ has disarmed; we now deploy.**

Misread: "Because judgment is coming, I should rage against culture."

Better: Because judgment is coming, **I should offer mercy and truth** now, urged by love, not animated by spite (Jude 22–23, NIV).

Misread: "If God wins, my pain shouldn't hurt."

Better: Hope doesn't shrink pain; it locates it, inside a story where Jesus keeps every promise.

Practicing "Submit → Resist → Replace" in light of the end

Practicing **submit → resist → replace** takes on fresh clarity in light of the end. Start with **submission:** *"Jesus, the war's outcome is Yours. I place this hour under Your authority."* (James 4:7, NIV) Then move to **resistance:** *"In Your name I reject the lie that darkness gets the last word."* (1 Peter 5:9, NIV) And finally, **replace** the lie with kingdom-seeking habits, one small act of obedience, one word of witness, one song of joy (Matthew 6:33; Philippians 4:4, NIV). The verdict is written; vigilance is still required.

Field Drill (this week)

- **Endgame Psalm & Promise (5 minutes daily).** Read Psalm 27 aloud and pair it with one endofstory promise (Revelation 21:4; Romans 16:20; Revelation 20:10, NIV). Pray: "Lord, let tomorrow's verdict shape today's voice."
- **The "No Condemnation" reply.** When accusation spikes, answer **out loud** with Romans 8:1 (NIV), then text an ally one sentence: "Light > lies, stood on 8:1."
- **Hope assignment.** Choose one person far from God. Pray Revelation 5:5 over them, **"See, the Lion of the tribe of Judah... has triumphed."** (NIV) Send a note, set a lunch, or serve them this week.
- **Quiet the frenzy, keep the flame.** Pick one 24hour window to sabbath the scroll. Replace doomscrolling with a slow walk and a short prayer list. **Preparation isn't panic; it's love in advance.**

REFLECTION & APPLICATION

- Where has uncertainty about the end produced either panic or passivity in you, and what truth above recalibrates your posture?

- Which of the four "Why the end matters now" points (courage, endurance, sobriety, hope) do you most need this month, and what practice will you pair with it?

- What accusation returns on repeat at night? Write your **Scripture answer** and practice speaking it aloud for seven days.

- Who near you needs your steady witness because the clock is running, and what will your first step be before Friday?

The stadium clock keeps ticking, but the outcome is not in doubt. The adversary will be silenced; the saints will be safe; the King will be seen. Until then, **lift your eyes, lock your shield with your people, and keep moving in obedience**. The lion still roars, but the **Lion of Judah** reigns, and **His triumph is the atmosphere in which you endure, resist, and rejoice. "The God of peace will soon crush Satan under your feet."** (Romans 16:20, NIV)

"SEE, THE LION OF THE TRIBE OF JUDAH, THE ROOT OF DAVID, HAS TRIUMPHED."

CHAPTER 14

THE LION OF JUDAH: OUR TRUE CHAMPION

The handler at Sarasota's Big Cat Habitat grinned when we asked how close we were to the lions. "Closer than your ears think," he said, and then, without warning, the air shook. The first roar didn't sound like sound; it felt like pressure in the ribs. A second followed, longer and deeper, and every kid on the rail fell silent. The handler wasn't rattled. "That's a territorial call," he explained. "It carries for miles. The message isn't 'I'm hunting you'; it's 'I rule here.'" I stood there thinking about how a roar changes a landscape long before you see the lion, and how the gospel announces a louder reality still. **There is another Lion whose voice doesn't terrorize His people; it steadies them.** He is not the prowler who devours; He is the King who delivers.

Scripture gives Him a name: **"See, the Lion of the tribe of Judah, the Root of David, has triumphed."** (Revelation 5:5, NIV) That line does more than crown a title; it declares a victory. The New Testament insists that Jesus isn't one spiritual option among many; **He is the reigning King whose triumph reframes the fight. "All authority in heaven and on earth has been given to me."** (Matthew 28:18, NIV) **Authority** is the key word, over sin and death, over hell and the grave, over your Tuesday and your future.

The enemy prowls, but Jesus presides.

The Story Behind the Name

The title "Lion of Judah" blooms from a long promise. Jacob's blessing over Judah foresaw a ruler whose scepter would not depart: **"You are a lion's cub, Judah… The scepter will not depart from Judah… until he to whom it belongs shall come."** (Genesis 49:9–10, NIV) That royal line runs through David to Christ, and Revelation picks up the thread, not to introduce a predator, but to enthrone a Savior.

What happens when heaven looks for the Lion? John hears *Lion* and turns and sees a *Lamb*. The vision is jarring by design: the One who reigns like a Lion **wins like a Lamb**, by selfgiving love at the cross. **"And having disarmed the powers and authorities, he made a public spectacle of them, triumphing over them by the cross."** (Colossians 2:15, NIV) **Power in the kingdom doesn't bludgeon; it bleeds for the beloved and breaks the back of evil.**

This is why the enemy's roar cannot be the loudest sound in a believer's life. **The cross is the decisive thunder; the resurrection is the echo that never stops.**

Lion vs. lion: Two very different roars

The Bible speaks of a roaring lion seeking someone to devour (1 Peter 5:8), and it also speaks of the Lion of Judah who has triumphed (Revelation 5:5). Confusing them is a category error with consequences. One roars to terrify; the Other rules to testify to declare that the kingdom has come near and the King is good.

The prowling lion **lies, accuses, divides, and distracts** (John 8:44; Revelation 12:10), while the reigning Lion **speaks truth, covers shame, makes peace, and sends His people on mission** (John 10:10; Romans 5:1; Matthew 28:18–20). He does not hunt His people; He holds them. He does not intimidate His Bride; He intercedes for her. Jesus is not merely in your corner; He is on the throne.

What the Lion's reign means for people in a world with teeth

If Jesus truly is the reigning Lion of Judah, then His kingship reshapes the way we live in a world with teeth. It gives us assurance, strength, hope, and a new center of gravity right now, not someday.

We receive **assurance in the now** because "all authority... has been given" to Jesus (Matthew 28:18, NIV). Fear no longer gets the final vote on your calendar or your calling. The psalmist's confidence becomes ours: "The Lord is my light and my salvation, whom shall I fear?" (Psalm 27:1, NIV) Christian confidence isn't self-talk; it's Savior assurance.

We also learn a **different kind of power**. The Lion reigns like a Lamb. His path to the throne ran through weakness for love's sake, and that pattern reshapes us. Scripture reminds us, "My power is made perfect in weakness." (2 Corinthians 12:9, NIV) We don't overpower to win; we out-love and outlast because He already overcame.

We gain **hope with teeth** as well. The King is not wringing His hands at history. "He must reign until he has put all his enemies under his feet." (1 Corinthians 15:25, NIV) That includes the patterns, powers, and personal lies that harass you at 11:30 p.m. Hope becomes courage when you remember who rules the room.

And lastly, the Lion's rule gives you **a new center of gravity**. If Jesus is the Lion, then attention belongs to Him: "Seek first his kingdom and his righteousness." (Matthew 6:33, NIV) Doom scrolling does not disciple you; Christ's kingship does. His authority becomes the weight that steadies your soul.

Holding Lion and Lamb together (so we don't shrink either)

Many of us tend to default toward one of two distorted pictures of Jesus. Some of us lean into a **sentimental Lamb and a silent Lion,** imagining a Savior who is only gentle, always agreeable, and never disruptive. But the true King flips tables, dethrones idols, and demands our allegiance. Others drift toward a **harsh Lion and a hidden Lamb**, envisioning Jesus as only severe, always demanding, and never tender. Yet this same King touches lepers, weeps at graves, and welcomes children.

Revelation heals the split. When John turns to see the Lion, he beholds a Lamb, looking as if it had been slain (Revelation 5:6). His authority is cruciform strength wrapped in sacrifice, and His roar carries mercy.

So, when you feel cornered by sin, remember: He is strong enough to break its power and gentle enough to carry you through the struggle. And when you feel small before cultural headwinds, remember: He is kingly enough to steady you and kind enough to shepherd you.

Living under a real King (habits of allegiance)

Allegiance is not a feeling; it is a rhythm, a way of ordering your life so the Lion of Judah stays at the center of your week. One way to practice this is through a **daily enthronement prayer**, just two minutes before email or errands: *"Jesus, You have all authority"* (Matthew 28:18, NIV). *"I place this day under Your rule. Let Your Word define, Your Spirit direct, Your love govern."* Then read a short psalm aloud. Worship resets your weight; your weight lands on His rule.

Another rhythm is a **weekly table of remembrance**. Choose one meal each week where your home answers two simple questions: *"Where did we see the King's kindness?"* and *"Where did we join His work?"* This keeps the Kingdom from becoming abstract and turns it into attention.

A third rhythm is the practiced cadence of **submit resist replace**. We've woven this throughout the book, but under the Lion's reign it carries particular authority (James 4:7, NIV). Submit to the King's rule; resist the dark whisper; replace the pull with a King-shaped action Scripture spoken, service given, gratitude named. Allegiance sounds like obedience in small things.

Finally, build in a **monthly generosity act that costs you**. Kings fund missions; citizens of the King do too. Choose to give in a way that re-teaches your heart who God is and who He is not. Generosity becomes allegiance with receipts.

The King's voice vs. the Accuser's noise (a discerner you can use today)

Ask of every inner narration: *Is this the King's cadence or the enemy's clamor?*

- **King Jesus: draws** with conviction and a clear next step; **the Accuser: drives** with shame and vague doom. (John 10:27, NIV)
- **King Jesus: names truth** and **offers grace; the Accuser: twists truth** and **weaponizes guilt**. (Romans 8:1, NIV)
- **King Jesus: sends** you toward people; **the Accuser: isolates** you from them. (Hebrews 10:24–25, NIV)

If you cannot pray a sentence and then obey a step, you are not hearing the King.

Case windows: what it looks like to live lion-centered

To see how this takes shape in real lives, here are a few snapshots of what it looks like when ordinary people begin living with the Lion of Judah at the center.

A small business owner under pressure.

Receivables lagged; anxiety surged. Instead of micromanaging from fear, she began each morning with the enthronement prayer (Matthew 28:18), named one generous act each week, and practiced the submitresistreplace cadence when worry spiked. The numbers didn't heal overnight, but her presence did: steadier words, clearer decisions. **Authority above her replaced anxiety within her.**

A teenager in identity crosswinds.

The online voices were many; the King's voice became the anchor. Together with a mentor, she memorized **"See what great** love the Father has lavished on us, that we should be called children of God!" (1 John 3:1, NIV), deleted the most corrosive accounts, and served weekly on a kids' team. **The Lion's love gave her a name louder than the feed.**

A small church feeling cultural headwinds.

Headlines flared; attendance dipped. The elders led a month of Revelation 5 readings and weekly communion, repeated this refrain, **"We will name the enemy, but we will magnify Christ"**, and invited the body into tangible peacemaking in the city. The roar outside stayed loud; **the room learned to sing over it.**

Common misreads, and the better story

Misread: "If Jesus is King, I should never feel weak."

Better: The King **meets** you in weakness and **manifests** His power there (2 Corinthians 12:9, NIV).

Misread: "Because Christ has triumphed, resistance is optional."

Better: Christ's triumph **assigns** you to resistance, **"Submit... Resist the devil, and he will flee from you."** (James 4:7, NIV)

Misread: "Lion means loud."

Better: The King's roar can steady as a **whisper. "My sheep listen to my voice... and they follow me."** (John 10:27, NIV)

Misread: "Kingship is abstract doctrine."

Better: Kingship is **Tuesday**, how you answer an email, pay an invoice, forgive a friend, curate inputs, and **seek first His kingdom.** (Matthew 6:33, NIV)

When the night is long (and you need the end of the story)

Some nights, the enemy's snarl feels nearer than the King's song. Open the last pages: **"Now have come the salvation and the power and the kingdom of our God, and the authority of his Messiah."** (Revelation 12:10, NIV) and **"The devil... was thrown into the lake of burning sulfur."** (Revelation 20:10, NIV) The scoreboard is not ambiguous. **We fight present battles inside a settled war.** So keep praying, keep serving, keep standing. **"Stand firm. Let nothing move you. Always give yourselves fully to the work of the Lord."** (1 Corinthians 15:58, NIV)

We don't fight for victory; we fight from it, under the Lion's banner.

Field Drill (this week)

- **Daily enthronement (2 minutes).** Pray Matthew 28:18–20 in your own words. Name one decision you will place explicitly under Jesus' rule today. Speak **Psalm 27:1** aloud when fear flares.

- **One allegiance act.** Choose one concrete obedience that costs you, an apology you owe, a gift you've delayed, a boundary you need. **Allegiance sounds like action.**

- **Submit → Resist → Replace, Lion edition.** When a lie hits, say: "King Jesus, I submit this moment to **Your** authority." Resist the lie aloud. Replace it with a verse and a step of love. (James 4:7; John 10:10, NIV)

- **Table of remembrance.** At week's end, name two places you saw the King's kindness and one place you joined His work. Write them down; share them with someone.

- **Worship as warfare.** Sing one song that exalts Christ's reign each day. Let your mouth tutor your mood (Philippians 4:4, NIV).

REFLECTION & APPLICATION

- Where have you been treating Jesus more like a consultant than a King, and what specific practice will reenthrone Him this week?

- Which aspect of His rule do you most need right now, His **strength** (Lion) or His **tenderness** (Lamb)? How will you seek it?

- What "allegiance act" (generosity, confession, reconciliation, mission) will you take within 48 hours to say with your life, "Jesus reigns here"?

- Which voice has been loudest lately, the Accuser's or the ShepherdKing's, and how will you curate your inputs to keep Christ's voice clear?

At the habitat fence, that roar rearranged the air before we ever saw the mane. The handler called it a territorial claim, **a sound that tells the savannah who rules here**. Lift your eyes: a greater voice has filled the world. In the cross and empty tomb, the **Lion of Judah** has announced His reign, and His Spirit has made that reign present in you. So step out of the brush and into the open under His banner, **eyes up, heart steady, feet ready**, and let the King's victory set your pace. **"In all these things we are more than conquerors through him who loved us."** (Romans 8:37, NIV)

THE ONE WHO IS IN YOU IS
GREATER THAN THE ONE WHO
IS IN THE WORLD.

CHAPTER 15

LIVING VICTORIOUSLY EVERY DAY

At first light, the Ringling Bridge looked like a pale ribbon across Sarasota Bay. The water was glass, the gulls were talkative, and a small knot of runners stretched hamstrings near the starting cones. A volunteer checked watches and smiled: "You don't win a race at the start; you win it with a steady cadence." When the horn sounded, the crowd surged, but the best runners didn't sprint. Heads up, breath measured, they settled into rhythm. Half a mile in, my body learned what my head already knew: **victory isn't a single moment; it's a way of moving.**

That's the heartbeat of this closing chapter. The enemy still prowls, yes, but the **Lion of Judah** reigns. Our task is not to manufacture a dramatic finish every day; it's to carry a Christ-centered cadence into ordinary Tuesdays. Earlier, we said it this way: **real threats demand real adjustments**, and those adjustments become your rhythm.

The victory you live from, not for

The gospel plants you on settled ground. Paul says Jesus **"disarmed the powers and authorities"** and **"triumphed over them by the cross."** (Colossians 2:15, NIV) John adds the steadying counterpoint: **"The one who is in you is greater than the one who is in the world."** (1 John 4:4, NIV) Which means your daily posture is neither denial of the battle nor despair about the outcome. It's a third, better way: **alert confidence.**

Peter sketches that way in a single paragraph we've returned to all along: **"Humble yourselves... under God's mighty hand... Cast all your anxiety on him because he cares for you. Be alert and of sober mind... Resist him, standing firm in the faith... And the God of all grace... will himself restore you and make you strong, firm and steadfast."** (1 Peter 5:6–10, NIV) That paragraph is a training plan, not a Twitter quote.

You don't achieve victory; you inhabit it. Cadence isn't bravado; it's belonging, to Christ, to His people, to His promises.

A Tuesday cadence from 1 Peter 5 (five moves you can actually carry)

Think of these as the five beats of your stride. Not tasks to check, but a way to move through a day.

1) Humble, start low under God's hand.

"Humble yourselves, therefore, under God's mighty hand." (v. 6, NIV) Beginning low is not selfloathing; it's sanity. You acknowledge limits, invite leadership, and trade whiteknuckle control for trust. **Humility is the doorway where the rest of grace walks in.**

2) Cast, transfer the weight, don't glorify it.

"Cast all your anxiety on him because he cares for you." (v. 7, NIV) We practiced this: name the care, kneel your will, throw the burden onto Christ, then **replace** the empty space with Scripture and a small step. **Anxiety is a weight to cast, not a cross to carry.**

3) Alert, eyes open, mind clear.

"Be alert and of sober mind." (v. 8, NIV) This isn't jittery suspicion; it's **gospelcentered attentiveness**. Ask through the day: *What has my attention? What is this moment? What is my next faithful step?* We called it a lionawareness mindset, **awake because you are loved and sent.**

4) Resist, stand where you already belong.

"Resist him, standing firm in the faith." (v. 9, NIV) Resistance isn't volume; it's position. You submit to Jesus' authority (first), say

no to the specific lie (next), and **replace** the pull with a truth and a practice. **Submit → resist → replace** remains your simple, portable order of battle.

5) Expect, God himself will restore you.

"The God of all grace… will himself restore you and make you strong, firm and steadfast." (v. 10, NIV) That promise keeps your cadence joyful. **Hope doesn't shrink pain; it locates it, inside a story God has already secured.**

Triplebraided strength: Word, prayer, people

A rope is strong because its strands are intertwined, and your daily victory holds the same way only when the right strands stay braided together. First is the **Word**, because Scripture is not decor; it is direction and defense. "Your word is a lamp for my feet, a light on my path." (Psalm 119:105, NIV) Read it aloud somewhere you actually live, in the kitchen, on your commute, or in the parking lot.

Second is **prayer**, not as a last resort but as the very atmosphere you breathe. "Devote yourselves to prayer, being watchful and thankful." (Colossians 4:2, NIV) Watchfulness keeps you sane; gratitude keeps you soft.

And third is **people**, because lone saints become easy prey. Scripture urges us, "Let us… not give up meeting together… but encourage one another." (Hebrews 10:25, NIV) As we've said earlier, isolation promises relief, but it produces vulnerability. Lock shields.

The Word steadies your mind. Prayer softens your heart. People strengthen your hands.

A simple rule of life you can actually keep

From Nehemiah we learned to **pray and post a guard**, presence with a plan. (Nehemiah 4:9, NIV) Here's a lean trellis (no perfectionism, just persistence):

Daily (the 4 M's):

- **Morning, Word before world.** One psalm aloud; one sentence of prayer. **"Let the morning bring me word of your unfailing love…"** (Psalm 143:8, NIV)
- **Mealtimes, turn tables into altars.** Ask, *Where did you see God at work today?* (Deuteronomy 6:7, NIV)
- **Media, curate on purpose.** Apply **Philippians 4:8** to your feeds.
- **Margin, breathe on purpose.** A fiveminute midafternoon "watch & pray" walk (Matthew 26:41, NIV).

Weekly (the 4 A's):

- **Assemble** in worship (Hebrews 10:25, NIV).
- **Abide** in a screenlite Sabbath block (Isaiah 30:15, NIV).
- **Account** with an ally (James 5:16, NIV).
- **Active mercy**, serve someone (Hebrews 10:24, NIV).

Monthly (the 4 R's):

- **Review** where drift tried to start (Hebrews 2:1, NIV).
- **Repent** quickly (1 John 1:9, NIV).
- **Reorder** one commitment to match your calling (Ephesians 5:16, NIV).
- **Remember** God's kindness, write three answered prayers (Psalm 103:2, NIV).

None of that is flashy. All of it is **faithful**. And faithful is how victory feels on a Wednesday.

Four moments that often steal the cadence (and how to answer them)

Life has a way of interrupting even the best cadence, and certain moments tend to steal your stride more quickly than others. When those moments hit, here is how to respond with gospel reflex rather than exhaustion or panic.

When fear narrows your obedience, move your gaze from storm to Savior. Pray the three-line breath, *Jesus, You are with me… I cast this care…* and then speak Psalm 27:1 aloud: *"The Lord is my light and my salvation, whom shall I fear?"* Take one courageous step, whether it's sending the email or making the call. As we named earlier, confidence isn't noise; it's trust in motion.

When hurry thins your soul, name the lie: *Everything depends on me.* Answer it with God's steadying word: *"In quietness and trust is your strength."* (Isaiah 30:15, NIV) Carve out ten minutes for unhurried prayer and put Scripture before screens. Let pace become obedience, not panic.

When shame tells you to hide, refuse to curate your image, confess your reality. Scripture speaks stronger than shame: *"There is now no condemnation for those who are in Christ Jesus."* (Romans 8:1, NIV) Text your ally: *"Ground is tilting, can we talk?"* Confession breaks the spell; community keeps it broken.

When secrecy feels reasonable, remember what we learned about isolation: it's a trap disguised as rest (Hebrews 10:24–25; Ecclesiastes 4:12, NIV). Choose a small, stubborn re-entry show up even if you're quiet, sit in the row, say yes to coffee. Presence is a practice, not a personality type.

"Submit → Resist → Replace" in the wild (four everyday prototypes)

Here's what this rhythm looks like when the rubber meets the road, four everyday moments where *submit → resist → replace* becomes more than theory.

Temptation at 11:30 p.m.
Submit: "Jesus, this hour is under Your rule." (James 4:7, NIV)
Resist: "No, not tonight." Name it.
Replace: Phone on kitchen charger; Psalm aloud; text an ally. (1 Corinthians 10:13, NIV)

Comparison at 7:15 a.m.

Submit: "Father, my calling is from You."

Resist: "I reject the lie that worth = metrics."

Replace: Memorize **"A person can receive only what is given them from heaven."** (John 3:27, NIV); send one encouragement to the person you're tempted to resent.

Conflict at 3:40 p.m.

Submit: "Set a guard over my mouth." (Psalm 141:3, NIV)

Resist: Don't rehearse the worst story.

Replace: Speak slowly; name your part; **"as far as it depends on you, live at peace with everyone."** (Romans 12:18, NIV)

Fatigue at 9:05 p.m.

Submit: "I'm human; You are God."

Resist: The urge to doomscroll.

Replace: Tenminute gratitude walk; **"Give thanks in all circumstances."** (1 Thessalonians 5:18, NIV)

Your household as a haven (not a bunker)

All through this journey we framed vigilance as **love**, not paranoia. In a home, that looks like **Word before world** at breakfast, **table gratitude** at dinner, **fast confession and quick forgiveness**, and a shared, simple media plan shaped by **Philippians 4:8**. We called this earlier a "family safety plan," not because you're building walls of fear, but because **you're building reflexes of grace. What you normalize in peacetime determines how you respond in battle.**

When you wobble (because sometimes you will)

You won't always feel fast or brave. David didn't. Peter didn't. Elijah didn't. The gospel's answer isn't **try harder**, it's **come nearer. "Consider how far you have fallen! Repent and do the things you did at first."** (Revelation 2:5, NIV) That's not nostalgia; that's repair. Return to the early practices that woke your heart, Word before world, honest prayer, a table with believers, and let the Spirit put breath back in your stride. **Grace doesn't excuse sin; grace equips you to stand up and walk again.** (1 John 1:9, NIV)

Mission in motion (because victory loves to move)

We haven't just been learning how to **survive**; we've been training to **serve**. The New Testament cadence lands here: **"Be on your guard; stand firm in the faith; be courageous; be strong. Do everything in love."** (1 Corinthians 16:13–14, NIV) Your neighbors don't need a lecture on lions; they need a living picture of a steady life under a better King. **Worship, then work; pray, then post the guard; confess, then comfort; resist, then bless.** That's how light travels down a street.

A benediction for the road

Lift your eyes: the prowling lion still roars, but **the Lion of Judah** still reigns. His cross has already thundered; His Spirit already indwells; His promises already hold. Walk the bridge again tomorrow, head up, breath measured, **eyes on the One who carries your weight**. And let Peter's sentence keep time with your steps: **"Cast all your anxiety on him because he cares for you."** (1 Peter 5:7, NIV) **Care is the cadence; Christ is the strength.**

Field Drill (this week)

- **90-second morning suitup.** Pray 1 Peter 5:6–10 in your own words: *humble → cast → alert → resist → expect restoration.* Speak one "faith headline" aloud (Psalm 27:1; Matthew 28:20; Matthew 6:33, NIV).
- **Twopocket card.** Left card: *My part today* (one obedient step). Right card: *God's part* (outcomes I cannot control). At lunch, swap back anything you grabbed from His pocket.

- **CPR group text (Celebrate / Pressure / Request).** With two allies, rotate a threeline checkin every other day. Pray brief, specific prayers for one another. (Hebrews 10:24–25; James 5:16, NIV)

- **Screen Sabbath (halfday).** Put devices in a basket; put people in the room. Take a slow walk and pray **Philippians 4:6–7** with your steps.

- **One mission move.** Choose a neighbor or coworker and deliver a tangible encouragement (a note, a meal, a prayer). Let love turn vigilance into blessing. (1 Corinthians 16:14, NIV)

REFLECTION & APPLICATION

- Which beat of the 1 Peter 5 cadence, **humble, cast, alert, resist, expect**, needs the most practice this week, and what small change will you make by tonight?

- Where does your rope feel thin, **Word, prayer, or people**, and how will you rebraid that strand in the next seven days?

- Which moment most steals your cadence, fear, hurry, shame, or secrecy, and which **submit → resist → replace** script will you carry into it?

- What single "mission move" will turn your vigilance outward this week, and who will you invite to do it with you?

You can't win the whole race at mile one. But you can carry the right cadence at mile one, and at mile two, and at mile ten. That's how finish lines are crossed: **not with panic or pose, but with practiced trust.** So step forward under **"the God of all grace"** who **"will himself restore you and make you strong, firm and steadfast."** (1 Peter 5:10, NIV) The lion still prowls, but saints who live awake, anchored, and **together** are hard to devour and a joy to the King. And the King is with you. Always.

VOICE DISCERNER: "DRAWS VS. DRIVES"

Purpose: A quick filter to test impressions, self-talk, cultural messages, or counsel you're hearing.

How to use: Read down each row. Which column best matches the tone, fruit, and direction of the voice you're sensing?

The Shepherd's Voice (Draws)	The Accuser's Voice (Drives)
Leads with **love** and *specific conviction* that names the sin and points to a way back.	Pushes with **guilt/shame,** often vague and sweeping ("you're just a failure").
Pulls you closer to Jesus and into healthy community.	**Pushes you away** from Jesus and isolates you from others.
Brings **clarity** anchored in Scripture and wise counsel.	Breeds **confusion** and constantly shifts the target.
Offers **grace and hope:** repentance is possible, restoration is real.	Announces **doom:** "There's no way back for you."
Produces **peace** that steadies, even when challenging.	Produces **panic** or pressure to fix everything *right now.*
Speaks **truth** that aligns with the whole counsel of God's Word.	**Twists** truth (half-truths, prooftexts, "angel of light" vibes).
Invites **humility, confession, and growth.**	Stokes **pride** or selfloathing anything but repentance.
Encourages **perseverance** and patient obedience.	**Hurries** you into rash, reactive decisions.

The Shepherd's Voice (Draws)	The Accuser's Voice (Drives)
Builds and **edifies**; correction feels surgical, not savage.	**Tears down** your identity and worth in Christ.
Names real issues with **specific next steps.**	Stays **nebulous** lots of accusation, no path forward.
Leads to **worship, gratitude, and courage.**	Fuels **fear, cynicism, and despair.**
Keeps you **submitted to God,** so resistance has power.	Keeps you **selfreliant,** so resistance rings hollow.

Three-Step Discernment (60 seconds):

1. Submit to God afresh ("Jesus, I yield every part of me to You").

2. Screen the voice with the grid above note which column it matches most.

3. Stand on Scripture and take the next obedient step you *do* know to take.

Scripture anchors to pair with this card:

- *"Be alert and of sober mind."* (1 Pet. 5:8)
- Jesus calls the devil *"a liar and the father of lies."* (John 8:44)
- *"Satan masquerades as an angel of light."* (2 Cor. 11:14)
- *"Put on the full armor of God... against the devil's schemes."* (Eph. 6:11)
- *"Submit yourselves... to God. Resist the devil, and he will flee."* (James 4:7)

7DAY "SOBER JOY" DEVOTIONAL

Day 1: Awake, Not Afraid

Read: **"Be alert and of sober mind..."** (1 Peter 5:8, NIV)

Prayer: *Jesus, wake me to what's real; anchor me in Your care.*

Day 2: Submit → Resist → Replace

Read: **"Submit yourselves, then, to God. Resist the devil, and he will flee from you."** (James 4:7, NIV)

Practice: Name one pressure today; submit it, resist the lie, replace with one Scripture.

Day 3: Word Before World

Read: **"Your word is a lamp for my feet, a light on my path."** (Psalm 119:105, NIV)

Practice: Read one psalm aloud before your phone.

Day 4: Guard the Gate

Read: **"Above all else, guard your heart..."** (Proverbs 4:23, NIV)

Practice: Write one if/then predecision for your weak spot.

Day 5: Don't Walk Alone

Read: **"A cord of three strands is not quickly broken."** (Ecclesiastes 4:12, NIV)

Practice: Text an ally: "Ground is tilting, check in this week?"

Day 6: Cast, Don't Carry

Read: **"Cast all your anxiety on him because he cares for you."** (1 Peter 5:7, NIV)

Practice: Twopocket card, my part vs. God's part.

Day 7: Confidence Over Fear

Read: **"The Lord is my light and my salvation, whom shall I fear?"** (Psalm 27:1, NIV)

Prayer: *Spirit of power, love, and a sound mind, steady me; send me.*

SPIRITUAL WARFARE FIELD GUIDE

1) Morning liturgy (90 seconds).

"Humble yourselves... Cast all your anxiety on him... Be alert... Resist... And the God of all grace... will himself restore you." (1 Peter 5:6–10, NIV)

Pray the "SuitUp" (Belt of Truth... Sword of the Spirit). **"Put on the full armor of God..."** (Ephesians 6:11, NIV)

2) The moment a pressure hits: the 4step drill.

- **Name it** (fear, lure, accusation, confusion).
- **Kneel/Submit:** *Jesus, I place this under Your authority.* **"Submit yourselves, then, to God."** (James 4:7, NIV)
- **Cast it:** *I throw this care onto You.* **"Cast all your anxiety on him because he cares for you."** (1 Peter 5:7, NIV)
- **Replace it:** speak Scripture, take one embodied step (step outside; text an ally; serve). **"The peace of God... will guard your hearts..."** (Philippians 4:7, NIV)

3) The voice test (fast discerner).

The Shepherd's voice **draws** with conviction and a next step; the enemy's voice **drives** with shame and doom. **"My sheep listen to my voice."** (John 10:27, NIV)

4) Three "faith headlines" to carry.

- Provision: **"Seek first his kingdom..."** (Matthew 6:33, NIV)
- Identity: **"See what great love the Father has lavished on us..."** (1 John 3:1, NIV)
- Fear: **"The Lord is my light and my salvation, whom shall I fear?"** (Psalm 27:1, NIV)

5) Two guardrails that change Tuesdays.

- **Word before world** (Scripture before screens).
- **Don't walk alone** (two allies, weekly 20minute checkin). **"Carry each other's burdens..."** (Galatians 6:2, NIV)

6) Evening examen (3 minutes).

Where did I carry, not cast? Where did God carry me? **"Give thanks in all circumstances."** (1 Thessalonians 5:18, NIV)

Short prayer to close:

King Jesus, You have all authority. **Greater is He who is in me than he who is in the world.** *(1 John 4:4, NIV) Strengthen me to submit, resist, and replace, today. Amen.*

B elow, you will find the "I Am List" which is a personal favorite of mine, and I've chosen to include it at the end of this book as a reminder of who you are in Christ. These truths, straight from Scripture, are meant to anchor your identity not in how you feel or what the world says but in what God has declared about you. I encourage you to read through them slowly, reflect on each one, and look up the verses in your own Bible. Let this list be a tool for self-reflection, spiritual growth, and encouragement. Whether you use it in personal devotion, prayer, or Bible study, may these truths help you walk more confidently in your identity as a beloved child of God.

I AM LIST

I am a child of God.
Romans 8:16; 1 John 3:1,2

I am saved by grace through faith.
Ephesians 2:8

I am redeemed from the hand of the adversary.
Psalms 107:2

I am an heir of eternal life.
1 John 5:11-12

I am forgiven.
Ephesians 1:7

I am led by the Spirit of God.
Romans 8:14

I am a new creature.
2 Corinthians 5:17

I am redeemed from the curse of the law.
Galatians 3:13

I am carried through by God Himself.
Isaiah 46:4

I am strong in the Lord and in His mighty power.
Ephesians 6:10

I am living by faith and not by sight.
2 Corinthians 5:7

I am rescued from the dominion of darkness.
Colossians 1:13

I am justified.
Romans 5:1

I am an heir of God and a co-heir with Christ.
Romans 8:17

I am blessed with every spiritual blessing.
Ephesians 1:3

I am an overcomer by the blood of the Lamb and the word of my testimony.
Revelation 12:11

I am the light of the world.
Matthew 5:14

I am an imitator of God, as a beloved child, to walk in Jesus' love.
Ephesians 5:1

I am healed by His wounds.
1 Peter 2:24

I am being transformed by the renewing of my mind.
Romans 12:2

I am heir to the blessings of Abraham.
Galatians 3:14

I do all things through Christ who strengthens me.
Philippians 4:13

I am more than a conqueror.
Romans 8:37

I am blameless and free from accusation.
Colossians 1:22

Christ, Himself, is in me.
Colossians 1:27

I am firmly rooted in Jesus, and I am being built up in Him.
Colossians 2:7

I have been made complete in Jesus.
Colossians 2:10

I have been spiritually circumcised; my old unregenerate nature
has been removed.
Colossians 2:10-13

I have been buried, raised, and made alive in Jesus.
Colossians 2:12,13

I died with Christ, and I have been raised up with Christ. My life is
now hidden with Christ in God. Christ is now my life.
Colossians 3:1-3

I am chosen of God, holy and dearly loved.
Colossians 3:12; 1 Thessalonians 1:4

I am a son of light and not of darkness.
1 Thessalonians 5:5

I have been given a spirit of power, love, and self-discipline.
2 Timothy 1:7

I have been saved and set apart according to God's doing.
2 Timothy 1:9; Titus 3:5

Because I am sanctified and I am one with the Sanctifier, He is not ashamed to call me brother.
Hebrews 2:11

I am a holy partaker of a heavenly calling.
Hebrews 3:1

I have the right to come boldly before the Throne of God to find mercy and grace in time of need.
Hebrews 4:16

I have been born again.
1 Peter 1:23

I am a living stone, being built up as a spiritual house for a holy priesthood, to offer up spiritual sacrifices acceptable to God through Jesus Christ.
1 Peter 2:5

I am a member of a chosen race, a royal priesthood, a holy nation, a people for God's own possession.
1 Peter 2:9,10

I am an alien and a stranger.
1 Peter 2:11

I am an enemy of the devil.
1 Peter 5:8

I have been given exceedingly great and precious promises by God by which I am a partaker of God's divine nature.
2 Peter 1:4

I am forgiven on account of Jesus' name.
1 John 2:12

I am anointed by God.
1 John 2:27

I am loved.
1 John 4:10

I have life.
1 John 5:12

I am born of God, and the evil one... the devil... cannot touch me.
1 John 5:18

I have been redeemed.
Revelation 5:9

My sinful nature, in Jesus, has been healed.
Isaiah 53:5

I am the salt of the earth.
Matthew 5:13

I am commissioned to make disciples.
Matthew 28:19,20

I am a child of God.
John 1:12

I have eternal life.
John 3:16

I have been given peace.
John 14:27

I am part of the true vine.
John 15:1-5

I am clean.
John 15:3

I am Jesus' friend.
John 15:15

I am chosen and appointed by Jesus to bear fruit.
John 15:16

I have been given glory, I am one with Jesus.
John 17:22

I have been justified.
Romans 5:1

I died with Christ and died to the power of sin's rule over my life.
Romans 6:1-6

I am a slave of righteousness.
Romans 6:18

I am free from sin and enslaved to God.
Romans 6:22

I am free from condemnation.
Romans 8:1

I am a son of God.
Romans 8:14-15; Galatians 3:26; Galatians 4:6

I am a joint heir with Christ.
Romans 8:17

I am more than a conqueror through Christ, who loves me.
Romans 8:37

I am given faith.
Romans 12:3

I have been sanctified and called to holiness.
1 Corinthians 1:2

I have been given grace.
1 Corinthians 1:4

I have been placed into Christ by God's doing.
1 Corinthians 1:30

I have received the Spirit of God into my life, that I might know the things given to me by God.
1 Corinthians 2:12

I have been given the mind of Christ.
1 Corinthians 2:16

I am a temple, a dwelling place of God. His Spirit and His Life dwell in me.
1 Corinthians 3:16; 1 Corinthians 6:19

I am united to the Lord, and I am one in spirit with Him.
1 Corinthians 6:17

I am bought with a price, I am not my own, I belong to God.
1 Corinthians 6:19-20; 1 Corinthians 7:23

I am called.
1 Corinthians 7:17

I am a member of Christ's body.
1 Corinthians 12:27; Ephesians 5:30

I am victorious.
1 Corinthians 15:57

I have been established, anointed, and sealed by God in Christ, and I have been given to the Holy Spirit as a pledge guaranteeing my inheritance to come.
2 Corinthians 1:21; Ephesians 1:13-14

I am led by God in Triumphal procession.
2 Corinthians 2:14

I am a fragrance of Christ to God among those who are being saved and among those who are perishing.
2 Corinthians 2:15

I am being changed into the likeness of Jesus.
2 Corinthians 3:18

I no longer alive for myself, but for He who died and rose again on my behalf.
2 Corinthians 5:14-15

I am a new creation.
2 Corinthians 5:17

I am reconciled to God, and I am a minister of reconciliation.
2 Corinthians 5:18-19

I have been made righteous.
2 Corinthians 5:21

I am well content with weaknesses, ...; for when I am weak, then I am strong.
2 Corinthians 12:10

I have been crucified with Christ, and it is no longer I who live, but Christ lives in me.
Galatians 2:20

I am a son of God through faith in Christ Jesus.
Galatians 3:26

I am Abraham's seed and heir of the promise from God.
Galatians 3:29

I am no longer a slave but a son; and if a son, then an heir
through God.
Galatians 4:6-7

I am a saint.
Ephesians 1:1; 1 Corinthians 1:2; Philippians 1:1; Colossians 1:2

I am blessed with every spiritual blessing.
Ephesians 1:3

I was chosen in Him before the foundation of the world, that I
would be holy and blameless before Him.
Ephesians 1:4

I am adopted as a son through Jesus Christ to Himself.
Ephesians 1:5

I am sealed in Him with the Holy Spirit of promise.
Ephesians 1:13

I am alive together with Christ.
Ephesians 2:5

I have been raised up with Him, and seated with Him in heaven.
Ephesians 2:6

I am His workmanship, created in Christ Jesus for good works.
Ephesians 2:10

I am a fellow citizen with the saints, and I am of God's household.
Ephesians 2:19

I have access in one Spirit to the Father.
Ephesians 2:18

I have boldness and confident access to God through faith in Him.
Ephesians 3:12

My citizenship is in heaven; seated with Him in the heavenly places in Christ Jesus.
Philippians 3:20; Ephesians 2:6

I am capable.
Philippians 4:13

I have been rescued from the domain of darkness and transferred to the kingdom of His beloved Son.
Colossians 1:13

I have been redeemed.
Colossians 1:14

I am better than I deserve.
Psalm 103:10-12

ABOUT THE AUTHOR

Dr. Nicholas Williams is the Amazon bestselling author of *How to Study the Bible, Be Free, When Fear and Faith Collide,* along with several *other books.* As the Lead Pastor at South Shore Community Church in Sarasota, Florida, Dr. Williams is passionate about sharing the transformative message of the gospel.

Dr. Williams holds a B.A., M.A.M., M.Div., and D.Min. from Luther Rice University. When he's not writing or leading his congregation, he enjoys traveling or being on the water with his wife, Lory, and their two children, Aubrie and Noah. You can learn more about his work and connect with him at **www.nic-williams.com** or on social media.

Instagram: **@pastornicwilliams**

www.ingramcontent.com/pod-product-compliance
Lightning Source LLC
Chambersburg PA
CBHW071514140726
47997CB00005B/1964